P9-DIF-603

UNDER TECHNOLOGY'S THUMB

UNDER TECHNOLOGY'S THUMB

William Leiss

HM
221
.L43
1990

McGill-Queen's University Press
Montreal & Kingston • London • Buffalo

© McGill-Queen's University Press 1990
ISBN 0-7735-0724-8 (cloth)
ISBN 0-7735-0748-5 (paper)

Legal deposit first quarter 1990
Bibliothèque nationale du Québec

∞

Printed in Canada on acid-free paper

INDIANA-
WITHDRAWN
PURDUE
LIBRARY

FORT WAYNE

6-9-92   P

Canadian Cataloguing in Publication Data

Leiss, William, 1939 –
    Under technology's thumb
    Includes index.
    Bibliography: p.
    ISBN 0-7735-0724-8
    1. Technology – Social aspects.
    2. Technological innovations – Social aspects.
    I. Title.
    HM 221.L34 1989   303.4'83   C89-090258-5

9-11-92

For Marilyn

CONTENTS

PREFACE

S ocieties are usually ambivalent about technical innovations, whether the novelties are steel axe-heads among New Guinea hill tribes or electronic transfers of funds in advanced industrialized societies today. The main reason for the ambivalence is that in most cases the advantages and disadvantages are inseparable: on introduction of innovations, some individuals or cultural practices will flourish and others will not.

For example, electronic transfers of funds will probably benefit most consumers, by providing greater convenience and flexibility in their banking transactions, as well as most banks, by reducing their operating costs in the long run. But some consumers also may be hurt if security provisions prove inadequate or if their privacy is violated through unauthorized access to electronic data banks. Some banks may be harmed if they cannot implement the new systems as efficiently as their competitors do. And, finally, some employees may lose their jobs and become either temporarily or permanently unemployed.

All economically advanced nations today have in place national and regional government policies for encouraging technological development. They do so in a variety of ways, especially by subsidizing costs of research and development (R&D) for new technologies through an elaborate network of tax incentive and grants programs. The chief rationale for all this is based on a two-step argument. First, many policy-makers believe that there is a demonstrable link between long-term economic growth and adequate levels of spending on R&D. On the assumption that almost everyone benefits to some degree from economic growth, it follows that there will be a collective advantage derived from spending enough on science and technology. Second, left to their own devices, private firms will underinvest in R&D, since they cannot capture all the revenue generated from further spin-off innovations based on their discoveries, and therefore governments put up a large share of the R&D funds so that the full social benefits derived from continued technical innovation can be won.

For those experiencing some negative effects from new technologies, however, it is small consolation to be told that there is a clear net social benefit, to wit, that the total set of benefits outweighs the comparable disbenefits. Therefore it is perfectly 'sensible' for those who believe (whether rightly or wrongly does not matter here) that they might be disadvantaged to oppose such developments, if they can, or at least to delay their implementation until someone offers them reasonable compensation. Those who attack new technologies often are called 'Luddites,' a label that stands for irrational and futile opposition to progress. Such a stance very well may be futile, but it is by no means irrational.

The main point is this: there is no fixed relation between new technologies themselves and the distribution of benefits and costs among persons and institutions. This is why we will always be somewhat ambivalent about new technologies even in a society such as the one we have today, which is explicitly devoted to the acceptance of scientific and technological progress. With each step forward, few of us can be certain about which side of the ledger we will fall on once the results are totted.

Given these uncertainties, it is offensive to be told that we must 'adapt' ourselves to new technologies. Technologies are instruments designed (ideally) to serve the purposes that we, as citizens living under conditions of political freedom, choose to place value on and to pursue. And although technological change forces itself on us, to some extent, by virtue of our integration into an international economic order, this situation does not and should not alter our resolve to choose freely our ultimate goals and purposes.

Sometimes our instruments do indeed appear out of control, like the broom in the tale of the sorcerer's apprentice. But this is an illusion. Even if we decide that we should support the process of technological innovation with the utmost vigour, we should remember that we retain the right and duty to shape the application and results of new technologies according to our values and our vision of the good society. And we have the duty to mitigate, so far as possible, the inevitable disadvantages stemming from those applications and experienced by some people at each step along the way.

I am greatly indebted to Philip J. Cercone, director of McGill-Queen's University Press, for his support and encouragement. Detailed comments by two readers for the Press, as well as John Parry's expert copy editing, resulted in many improvements to the manuscript.

Thanks are owed also to the editors who solicited my contributions to collections of essays on the topics taken up in this book: Gus Brannigan, Ted Chamberlin, Bill Dunn, Fred Fleron, Michael Mc-Grath, Paolo Rossi, Bernard Schiele, and David Shugarman. Chapters in this book are adapted from previously published material of mine, with kind permission of copyright holders: Marcel Dekker, Inc. (chapter 2); University of Toronto Press (3 and 7); Columbia University Press (4); Centre nationale des recherches scientifiques (5); *Scientia* (6); JAI Press, Inc. (8); and Greenwood Press, Inc. (9).[1] Several friends and colleagues greatly encouraged my continued work in these areas, for which they have earned special thanks: Gaëtan Tremblay (Université du Québec à Montréal), Arthur Kroker and Marilouise Kroker (Concordia), Heri Adam (Simon Fraser) Steve Kline (York), Ed Levy (British Columbia), and Neils Lind (Waterloo). Marike Finlay published a two-part essay about my writings on technology in the *Canadian Journal of Political and Social Theory*, 10 (1986), 174–95, and 11 (1987), 198–214.

Members of the Department of Communication at Simon Fraser University have provided an exceptionally supportive atmosphere for academic work; it is an honour to be associated with them. Professor Chad Day of Simon Fraser's Natural Resources Management Program gave me valuable guidance on the final draft of the manuscript. The many first-rate graduate and undergraduate students in the department are a source of inspiration. Anne Deslauriers entered the original essays into an electronic word-processing format that greatly facilitated my work; Ann Macklem and Suzanne Scheuneman were first-rate research assistants. Richard Smith's expert assistance with research questions as well as with computer software and hardware has aided my work beyond measure.

I am delighted to cite in the references books by Ian Angus and Sut Jhally, both now members of the Department of Communication at the University of Massachusetts at Amherst, that were originally written as doctoral theses under my supervision.

Finally, the development of my interests in public policy owes a great deal to my colleague, friend, and collaborator at Simon Fraser, Liora Salter, and not a little to some talented civil servants in Canadian federal government departments with whom I have had the pleasure to collaborate during the past few years: Frank Cedar and Wayne Ormrod (Agriculture); Russ Roberts (National Research Council and National Revenue); Dan Krewski, Len Ritter, and Neil Collishaw (Health and Welfare); and Hajo Versteeg (Pest Management Advisory Board).

PART ONE
THE TECHNOLOGICAL IMPERATIVE

1
INTRODUCTION:
THE IDOLS OF TECHNOLOGY

S tanding at the threshold of modern times, Francis Bacon saw in experimental science and technological innovation the keys to humanity's future. Human history to that point, he thought, was an endlessly repeated cycle of despair and false hopes. The false hopes were fed by the old illusion that a few cheap tricks and the right magical formulas would unlock nature's treasury, which contained unlimited wealth and power. The despair arose from humanity's seeming inability to escape from subjection to the natural forces that periodically visited famine, disease, pestilence, and destruction upon it. And that despair was perpetuated by established religion, with its fondness for handing out apparently endless punishments to Adam's descendants for the crimes committed in Paradise so long ago. The theologians of the day regarded these sinners as having already at their disposal quite sufficient means for doing mischief and so viewed as alarming and inadvisable the prospect of an enlarged human technological capacity.

And there was another source of despair: the routines of society and politics. To Bacon, society offered the depressing spectacle of equally undeserving sycophants competing for the available insignias of honour and preferment, along with the right to squander frivolously their disproportionate shares of the far-too-limited stock of material wealth. Politics was for him what we call today a 'zero-sum game,' where any person's success in advancing to greater power and influence inevitably was in direct proportion to his or her capacity to ruin someone else's fortunes in equal measure. These wastrels and experts in bureaucratic manoeuvring were so busy enhancing their own shares of the available spoils at the expense of others that they had no time for enlarging society's economic product as a whole.

Bacon was obsessed with the idea that all this could be changed, and so simply, if only society's rulers could be persuaded to champion his project for the conquest of nature by promoting the mechanical arts. He despised the condescending attitude toward the experimental sciences that pervaded the intellectual establishment of his day, and he tried to shock his contemporaries out of their complacency by insisting that the human mind, as well as human hands, required adequate technological 'instruments and machinery' for its work.[1] These comments introduced his great book, *The New Organon; or, True Directions concerning the Interpretation of Nature* (1620), in which Bacon tried to identify the obstacles that blocked the way to a scientific approach to the understanding of nature.

Those obstacles are epitomized in four types of 'idols.' For Bacon, the idols are 'false notions which are now in possession of the human understanding, and have taken deep root therein,' which work actively against true understanding of scientific method – a remarkable anticipation by him of the later concept of ideology. 'Idols of the tribe' stem from the inherent, universal structure of the human mind, such as the limited range of our senses, our tendency to draw conclusions from insufficient evidence, and our search for certainty in areas where there is no reasonable basis for it. 'Idols of the cave' arise from particular forms of culture and education that frame the outlooks of individuals and are expressed in particular prejudices; these cultural 'blinders' strongly influence our perceptions of events and channel our understanding of the world in ways designed to reinforce the hegemony of approved traditions.

'Idols of the marketplace are the most troublesome of all,' Bacon says. These are errors hidden in our languages themselves and come from the conventional usages of words as they evolve over time. Habitual modes of expression, which reflect past experiences of generations, are applied to new situations, and people using those expressions cannot see that the words do not describe the events to which they are being applied. Finally, 'idols of the theatre' are the false notions perpetuated by the great systems of thought, especially religion and philosophy, that dominate particular cultures and spawn dogmas that resist questioning and attempted refutation.[2]

In his utopian fantasy, *The New Atlantis*, Bacon imagined a setting in which obstacles to his program would be completely swept away. But even Bacon might have been astonished and made a little uneasy if he had known that Western society, within a few centuries, would be driven by purely secular ambitions and would elevate experimental science and technological innovation to a privileged position in its pantheon of public values. The great triumphs of science and technology are among the most cherished accomplishments of the modern age – and the sources of some of our new idols.

The idols of technology are the false notions that have grown up around modern society's fervent commitment to technological progress. First, sustained modern successes in technological innovation have given rise to systems of thought in which are embedded our own 'idols of the theatre.' We are given the impression that modern conditions compel us to make our values and institutions conform with those technologies themselves. We encounter statements to this effect all too frequently, for example, in discussions about the so-called information society. One Canadian federal government report on this subject states with a flourish: 'The advent of microelectronics is rapidly and irreversibly leading to a major and fundamental transformation of western society.' This is a good example of technological hyperbole – systematic and unwarranted exaggeration of the anticipated general social effects of new technologies. It is often matched by technological fetishism, which makes too much of new technologies, as if their features could magically transform our lives.

Second, there is the notion that our commitment to science and technology marks a qualitative break with all previous human history, which belief beguiles us into thinking that we are now immune from the 'superstitions' that ruled older civilizations. Our everyday language has become so saturated with technical jargon and scientific pronouncements that we pay too little attention to the autochthonous drives, expressed in the fear and hatred of peoples and customs different from our own, still humming deep within us. So the attempt to devise one of the very latest and most complex technologies imaginable, the so-called strategic defence initiative ('star wars') – which, if workable, would be a triumph of human ingenuity – was announced by the same leader who had earlier spoken of his determination to overcome an 'evil empire.' This deceptive quality of our everyday language expresses well our own 'idols of the marketplace.'

Third, every technological breakthrough is presented as a triumph for humanity in general, and thus we do not have to worry about the distribution of costs and benefits that attend its use. Those people affected by the introduction of new technologies traditionally have not been called to give evidence on its consequences, and we hear only about general increases in economic productivity and social welfare. This is especially true when, because of the structure of international trade, the benefits are confined largely to the innovating country and major negative effects are felt among nameless regions abroad. In this pervasive dissociation of techniques from their short-term (and long-term) social effects is found our own 'idols of the cave.'

And fourth, the undeniable achievements of modern science and technology, and their clear superiority over every earlier human approach to the investigation of natural forces, soon gave rise to an attitude of arrogant superiority toward all other ways of interpreting the human experience of the surrounding world. Beginning in the seventeenth century, this 'scientism' first set about stamping out its competitors among other systems of natural philosophy; by the nineteenth century it had turned its scorn on traditional religious, social, and ethical paradigms: The 'scientific method' would suffice, it was claimed, as the sole 'rational' approach to any and every question of values, social justice, and ultimate meaning. Scientism remains a lively and forceful part of our intellectual landscape, and the various modes of its expression represent our 'idols of the tribe.'[3]

Through the idols of technology we are led to believe that, if we hope to extract collective benefits from new technologies, we shall have to change our behaviour, in ways that we might not have done had we not felt compelled to do so. This vague sense of subjection to forces beyond our control is indeed the combined, overall effect of the four types of contemporary idols of technology. Since the promised benefits from technological progress can be substantial indeed, we are left with the impression that we are under technology's thumb.

The chapters to follow track these idols of technology through diverse sources and historical routes of development and assess where we stand in relation to them. Taken as a whole, they are framed thematically by considerations on the relation between knowledge and society: the results of scientific and technical discovery are usually presented as new ways of manipulating natural forces and materials so as to bring us practical benefits. Chapter 2 takes the story back to its origins in eighteenth-century political economy, where thinkers tried to come to grips with the social implications of the immense growth in the stock of technical knowledge that had begun to occur. The discussion shows that these considerations on the relation between knowledge and society, which continue down to the present, have left us with an ambiguous legacy. Is our stock of knowledge so immense and so specialized that only highly trained experts can understand it, and complex bureaucracies manage it? Or does the accumulated knowledge for the first time allow informed citizens to shape public policy?

Chapter 9 returns to this theme. The recently developed notion of the information society summarizes perfectly the long tradition that began with the eighteenth-century political economists: it portrays the creation and transfer of technical information (now heavily dependent on microelectronic technologies) as the main creator of economic value in an industrial economy. Champions of this idea urge us to do whatever is necessary to facilitate wider use of microelectronic technologies, so that we will not be 'left behind' in the race to create an information-intensive economy. This call to action, in which Bacon's old agenda resonates, forces us to confront our ambiguous legacy. We ought, I shall argue, to insist that government assist citizens in using the rapidly accumulating stock of technical knowledge to inform themselves about the choices that confront them and about the relation between those choices and the fundamental values of free and democratic societies.

Taken as a whole, therefore, this volume pursues a single theme: diagnosis of the powerful fatalism in our understanding of the relation between modern technologies and society and an attempted cure through establishment of a firm foundation, through an informed citizenry and enlightened public policies, for making choices about our future.

The belief that we are under pressure from the technological imperative cannot be just dismissed as a simple-minded mistake. The scope and pace of technological change have been and remain a looming presence among us, relentlessly throwing up new problems while the older ones are still being apprehended and long before they have been addressed at all adequately. We realize further that no individual industrialized nation can insulate its economic wealth against continued challenge from innovating forces elsewhere. Our institutional responses seem somehow predetermined and thus cannot be guided by choices grounded in enduring values.

To clarify the basis for choices we must first understand the pressures emanating from the technological imperative. The rest of part I (chapters 3–6) follows this strain of fatalism within some of the long-standing, pervasive hopes and fears based in our idols of technology. These fears and hopes have commingled since early modern times, with one side or the other sometimes more powerful for a while. All of them, composed of many and varied materials, rest on a common underlying structure: belief that the single most important determinant of the future is technological innovations and their social effects.

Chapters 3–6 contain one case study of each of the four idols of technology. Chapter 3 looks at an instance of the idols of the theatre: some widely accepted theories that envisage no escape from the technological imperative. Here we encounter a great number of extravagant claims about the overall impact of technology on social change. There are those who emphasize the beneficent aspects of this process, chiefly the expanding realm of personal choice and individual freedom which, it is claimed, flows from the results of technical innovation. At the other extreme, there are those who see modern technology as a corrosive force that penetrates and undermines the traditional institutions on which society depends.

Both views are fatalistic in that they regard social institutions as being forced to adjust to changes brought about by technological innovations, and both ignore or play down the reciprocal influence that conflicting social interests exert on the processes of technical innovation and application themselves. Neither formulation permits us to reconcile their widely divergent evaluations of the social significance of modern technologies. This chapter suggests a way out of the dilemma they have created: much greater precision about the key terminology which they both employ.

Chapter 4 considers responses to industrial technology and the factory system in some of the great imaginative literature of the nineteenth and early twentieth centuries. Passages in works by writers such as Emerson, Melville, and Ruskin illustrate well the operation of the 'idols of the market-place' in our understanding of technologies and their social effects. In Bacon's scheme, idols of the market-place stem from the way in which events are represented in language, and in nineteenth-century literature one can trace the responses to industrialism through the use of metaphors for the machine age.

The writers examined were struggling to comprehend the human consequences of industrial technology through the analogy of master and servant (that is, machines as the servants of humanity) – and saw the prospects for humanity, cast in these terms, as bleak, for this relationship seemed too easily reversible: the erstwhile servant would be master in the end. This reversal may appear rather simple-minded but was based on a profound observation: to reap the full benefits inherent in industrial technologies, humanity would have to scrap its traditional routines of everyday behaviour and adopt new ones, consistent with the organizational rhythm of industrial work (specialized function, regular hours of labour, adjustment to the speed of machine operations, and so forth). In other words, industrialism was not just about producing more and cheaper goods by harnessing clever machines to the service of humanity's desires. It was also about the corrosive effects of the machine on age-old ways of life, and the master-servant analogy concealed this fateful transition.

The idols of the cave, we may recall, arise from dissociation between the intrinsic characteristics of technologies themselves and the social effects flowing from their use. Chapter 5 presents the well-known modern theory of reification in this light. It opens with a remarkable passage from Marx's writings, in which Marx sought to capture the essential feature of industrialism that had made it such a radical break with earlier human history – namely, replacing human labour with machine functions as the actual core of the productive process. Whereas formerly the tool in the artisan's hand aided the plan of work in his or her mind, now the design of the machine itself incorporates humanity's accumulated technical ingenuity, and the worker (who is so much less skilled than the machine!) simply assists the machine in carrying out a plan of work without having any part in its conception.

According to the theory of reification, this 'inversion' of the relation between humanity and its instruments could be put right again only by a social revolution that replaced capitalism with socialism. My discussion of this influential theory seeks to show where the detailed diagnosis of the problem went wrong and thus why the proposed remedy would be ineffectual.

The subject-matter of chapter 6 fits nicely under the heading 'idols of the tribe.' Modern science and technology came to be regarded as the means by which humanity finally would assert its complete, rightful, and unchallengeable control over the forces of nature, yoking all of nature to the service of human needs. The early successes of the experimental sciences soon gave rise to the 'scientism' described earlier, which has used those successes and the practical benefits flowing therefrom to assert the pre-eminence of the natural sciences as the definitive interpreters of our experience of nature. The immense practical benefits attributed to science and technology have led many people to see the modern sciences as the sole measure for judging theories about the relation between humanity and nature.

The discussion in chapter 6 tries to show that this 'conceptual imperialism' is unhealthy for the sciences, as well as for our culture generally. We apprehend the world in varied ways, in accordance with different modes of judgment that correspond to different capabilities in the human mind. In the natural-science mode, we abstract from the sensuous experience of our surroundings in order to locate the common structure of matter-energy transformations. But the matter-energy fields represented by science ultimately in complex mathematical descriptions are only one form of our experience of nature. We apprehend the world in sensuous immediacy as well as in abstract mathematical forms, and neither approach can be regarded as providing better access to the 'reality' of nature. The sensuous appearance of nature is just as much an expression of its being as its hidden atomic structure is, if by its 'being' we mean its significance for us. We could not live in a world without sensuous qualities.

Differing modes of apprehending nature suggest the limitations of our practical scientific and technological ingenuity. The practical results of continued scientific discovery and technical innovation serve the purposes to which nations and peoples attach genuine importance – comfort and security, good health, leisure; or the glorification and service of the gods; or imperial domination over others. And, no matter what the level of scientific and technological ingenuity, societies need means for reassessing the purposes to be served by their collective choices and for examining the appropriateness of those purposes in the light of fundamental values such as justice, fairness, and compassion. The general outcome of part I is that we should not use the undeniable pressure of the technological imperative, which is felt throughout all institutions in contemporary societies, as an excuse for avoiding the need to make reasoned choices about our future.

Part II is concerned with the basis for making reasoned choices about the future. Chapter 7 picks up again the relation between humanity and nature. Environmental issues have two quite different aspects. Our uses of industrial technologies confront us with purely practical problems, to which we must find technical solutions – for example, disposing of hazardous chemical compounds in wastes by means of high-temperature incinerators. However, some environmental issues take us to the level of fundamental values – our treatment of domestic and laboratory animals, our responsibilities to future generations (when we squander non-renewable resources or store hazardous wastes), or preservation of wildlife species and their habitats.

Chapter 8 connects choices with a fundamental value (caring) that has been widely respected in our society for a long time. Making choices requires us to set priorities among all the individual and collective claims made on our attention and our resources, and our values allow us to assign priorities. Grounding choices in appropriate values is essential for public policies as well as for individual action.

Chapter 9 takes up the concept of the 'information society,' which recapitulates the themes of necessity and choice running through this book, and it is followed by a brief concluding chapter.

The treatment here does not extend to 'alternative technologies' – alternatives to the large-scale, energy-intensive technologies for resource extraction and goods production that tend to have (or carry a significant risk of) major adverse environmental effects. This neglect is not intended as disparagement of that subject, which is far too complex for passing comment. What we require at our present level of understanding is quite specific, case-by-case treatments. Such treatments must take into account managerial issues such as comparative economic benefits, environmental risk assessments, and employment aspects – as well as application of evaluation principles, grounded in theories of choices and values, to long-term implications for political, social, and cultural changes.[4]

I have instead devoted the following chapters to the more modest tasks of identifying the type of pressures that the technological imperative places on our social relations and marking the position from which we can successfully mount resistance to those pressures.

2
KNOWLEDGE AND POWER

The notion that technological innovation can qualitatively change social relations is a hallmark of modern thought, or 'modernity.' For Bacon, the essential promise of technology was not that it could address directly the traditional sources of human unhappiness but that it could gradually render them irrelevant. Envy, insecurity, and the striving for meaningless badges of social distinction would vanish in the universal celebrations over the material abundance and operational powers brought into being by science and technology's conquest of nature. Bacon saw much of the traditional failure to value scientific and technological innovation as rooted simply in intellectual confusion, what we call 'ideology.' People mired in such confusion, he believed, would appear more and more ludicrous in relation to the tangible increases in human welfare won by the new technology.[1]

Modes of production in pre-modern societies have relied on handicraft technologies, with agriculture at the centre of things, using primarily human and animal sources of energy. Like other aspects of society and culture, material production depends ordinarily on customs resistant to change. But the modern way that shattered this age-old pattern is dedicated to continuous change, as new knowledge about how natural forces act is applied systematically to technological innovation, which in turn leads to further discoveries and applications. For a long time the most dramatic success in this endeavour was machinery itself (including the integration of multiple machines into factory units) and the new sources of energy to drive it. Over time realization dawned that these were just particular manifestations of the more general, underlying basis for industrialism – the steady accumulation and integration of new technical knowledge. From this standpoint, technologies are essentially a crystallized form of human knowledge.

In this chapter I wish to illustrate some steps whereby this realization arose and developed. The story arrives at the present with a paradox in tow. An adequate supply of technical knowledge, it had been thought, would enable us to control and manage natural forces in the service of material production. This astonishing technological ingenuity, rooted in an ever more refined knowledge of natural forces and the structure of matter, casts into our laps previously unknown technological risks that turn out to be rather difficult to manage!

The chief risk is that of general nuclear war, which threatens to destroy not only human civilization but also the very biophysical environment in which human evolution occurred. The world's population watches in helpless anticipation as the leaders of the two nuclear superpowers try to reduce the surplus destructive capacities of their nuclear arsenals. Yet many 'peaceful' technologies, too, such as the widespread industrial uses of toxic chemical compounds, create risks that are inherently difficult to assess and manage. As I shall argue in chapter 10, the task of controlling such chemicals presents contemporary societies with complex administrative problems.[2]

In short, we have sought to reorder our relation to nature through industrial technologies and in so doing to escape the traditional human fate of being helpless victims of uncontrollable natural forces. Yet having taken great strides in this direction, we glimpse a similar prospect: once again, our technological apparatus appears to be, if not entirely beyond our control, at least remarkably resistant to serving in an unambiguous way the cause of human betterment. Is progress a circle, and the end just the beginning again?

The Social Function of Knowledge

The novel political theory and practice that arose in the early modern period in the West – often called classical liberalism – grounded its idea of social progress in the concept of rational or educated self-interest. Liberalism demanded dramatically expanded social and political freedom for individuals, because economic development depended on individuals having a generous territory within which to pursue their own interests. Liberalism further proposed that social constraints be limited primarily to protecting order, property, and the private observance of religion.

The political practice of early liberalism 'operationalized' this conception through a demand for effective enfranchisement of those who could demonstrate capacity for rationally understanding their interests. This principle was formulated by John Locke in straightforward terms: the rational person was the 'industrious' man who accumulated property.[3] Moreover, the public good was not to come about directly through operation of individual self-interest but rather was expected to result indirectly from the so-called natural harmony of private interests.

From its beginnings, liberal political theory was implicitly economic: 'Liberals came to assert not only that economics was the most useful form of knowledge for the individual in his pursuit of happiness, but that it also provided the necessary prescriptions for handling the common affairs of society.'[4] The theory of a self-regulating society, which emphasized the growth of individual rationality and advocated minimal interference by public institutional authority, was of course grounded in the theory of the self-regulating market-place. And this latter theory provided the link between cultivation of individual rationality and emerging recognition of the growing social importance of knowledge.

As the pursuit of rational self-interest became interwoven with an increasingly complex set of market relations, two things happened. First, more and more understanding was required of individuals who wished to master these complex relations and turn them to their own advantage. Thus the distribution of power, wealth, and status would change as a function of differential success by individuals and groups in adapting to this requirement. Knowledge itself gradually becomes an important commodity; those who are able to organize or manage its use derive the material benefits flowing therefrom.

Second, increasing instrumental use of knowledge in the pursuit of individual self-interest will result in the sedimentation of knowledge in society's accumulating productive resources. As the interests of society are more and more clearly identified with the expansion of those resources (in the form of fixed capital), society at large comes to have an interest in the growth of knowledge. Growing realization of this point is apparent in early modern political economy, where, in seeking to clarify what was required to ensure expansion of market relations, political economists recognized the important social function of knowledge.

In his study of seventeenth- and eighteenth-century economic literature, E.A.J. Johnson notes his agreement with the opinion prevailing during this period that 'the keys that can open the treasures of economic progress are therefore forged in the schoolroom, the laboratory, the inventor's shop, and the research institute.' He finds in the literature keen appreciation of the crucial importance of technical knowledge for economic progress. In these sources the word 'art' stands for what we now call knowledge, skill, and technical proficiency; in them 'art was ... conceived as an indispensable prerequisite for economic development, since it represents the "artificial means" whereby a progressive economy can improve its natural resources.'[5]

Much of classical (eighteenth-century) political economy maintained and deepened this insight, especially in sensing the value of general theoretical knowledge of every kind and in ranking knowledge among the primary components of society's 'capital.' For example, Adam Smith, itemizing in *The Wealth of Nations* (1776) the elements that compose the stock of fixed capital, includes the following: 'Fourthly, of the acquired and useful abilities of all the inhabitants or members of the society. The acquisition of such talents, by the maintenance of the acquirer during his education, study, or apprenticeship, always costs a real expense, which is a capital fixed and realized, as it were, in his person. These talents, as they make a part of his fortune, so do they likewise of that of the society to which he belongs.'[6]

During the nineteenth century, under the impact of accelerating scientific discovery and its successful technological application, political economists emphasized the unity of theoretical and practical knowledge and perceived its beneficial social consequences very broadly. For example, the French theorist J.-B. Say wrote: 'Academies, libraries, public schools, and museums, founded by enlightened governments, contribute to the creation of wealth, by the further discovery of truth, and the diffusion of what was known before; thus empowering the superior agents and directors of production, to extend the application of human science to the supply of human wants.'[7] And, likewise, John Stuart Mill in his *Principles of Political Economy* (1848): 'In a national, or universal point of view, the labour of the savant, or speculative thinker, is as much a part of production in the very narrowest sense, as that of the inventor of a practical art; many such inventions having been the direct consequences of theoretical discoveries, and every extension of knowledge of the powers of nature being fruitful of applications to the purposes of outward life.'[8]

These quotations are samples from an extensive literature. Concluding a comprehensive survey of the educational theory of political economists (from Adam Smith to modern historians of the subject, such as Edwin Cannan), Pierre Tu summarizes their common sentiment as follows: 'Education is a capital good in that it abridges labour: An educated man is usually more productive than an untrained worker. To the society as a whole, education also constitutes a stock of immaterial capital which is far more important than physical capital.'[9]

The General Intellect

These ideas were taken up also by Marx, with an exhaustive analysis and critique of the tradition of political economy. Marx criticized his predecessors for failing to see what he considered an anomaly, between detailed planning by individual capitalists for new productive forces, including methodical application of new knowledge, and the 'anarchic' structure of the market-place as a whole.

From society's standpoint, he argued, the growth of productive forces 'is again traceable in the final analysis to the social nature of labour engaged in production; to the division of labour in society; and to the development of intellectual labour, especially in the natural sciences.' Marx saw the social and economic effects of scientific and technological progress as being manifested in the growing productivity of labour; but productive applications of this progress (embodied in increasingly sophisticated machinery) end up as fixed capital, i.e. as private property.[10]

For Marx the expanding social role of knowledge in the productive process of industrial capitalism was a crucial feature of that system, and he returns to this point again and again in his writings. He thought that it would have broad social consequences, transcending the economic sphere: 'The development of fixed capital indicates to what degree general social knowledge has become a direct force of production, and to what degree, hence, the conditions of the process of social life itself have come under the control of the general intellect and been transformed in accordance with it.'[11] A productive system that depends on scientific knowledge and sophisticated technical skills widely diffused among workers thus raises the possibility, according to Marx, of a transformed society. I shall return to the 'general intellect' later in this chapter.

To summarize: first, in the evolution of political economy from the seventeenth to the nineteenth century, there is clear appreciation of the fact that knowledge represents a key productive resource. Many writers regarded scientific and technical knowledge as the cornerstone of the truly revolutionary changes in production made through the industrial system. Second, the specific importance of theoretical knowledge in the broadest sense was understood well by nineteenth-century political economists. Third, for Marx and other utopian thinkers, this incorporation and promotion of knowledge in the productive process marked a decisive step for society as a whole.

Naturally, classical political economy does not provide an adequate model for understanding industrialized societies today. In pre-Marx political economy, one finds only dim awareness of the broad social implications of knowledge being a key factor of production. However, Marx, who saw some of those implications, seriously underestimated the longevity of the new concatenation of productive factors within the framework of capitalist property relationships. Yet both the successes and the failures of earlier political economy contribute to a better understanding of the more recent commentaries discussed in the next section.

Technological Society

The theory of intellectual capital formulated during the past two decades claims to discern a qualitative difference between our society and its predecessors: 'Knowledge permeates the whole ethos and structure of technological society. This is what mainly distinguishes it from previous forms of society.'[12] Moreover, it is said that we are already conscious of this difference and encourage this ongoing transformation: 'Our society values the production and inculcation of knowledge more than ever before ... Our own age is characterized by a deliberate fostering of technological change and, in general, by the growing social role of knowledge.'[13]

The new social importance of knowledge is thought to be reflected not only in a rising level of general education and technical skills but also in structural (institutional) alteration in society, which is already the object of conscious management. This has been argued by, among others, John Kenneth Galbraith, in *The New Industrial State*: 'Given a competent business organization, capital is now ordinarily available. But the mere possession of capital is now no guarantee that the requisite talent can be obtained and organized. One should expect, from past experience, to find a new shift of power in the industrial enterprise, this one from capital to organized intelligence. And one would expect that this shift would be reflected in the deployment of power in the society at large ... Power has, in fact, passed to what anyone in search of novelty might be justified in calling a new factor of production. This is the association of men of diverse technical knowledge, experience or other talent which modern industrial technology and planning require.' Galbraith contends that the shift from capital to organized technical knowledge as the crucial factor of production is analogous to the earlier shift from land to capital and that important sociopolitical changes must ensure. The large corporation, as the basic economic unit, is the progeny of capital; but its own internal development leads it to encounter certain necessities (most important, long-range planning) that reduce the relative significance of capital and bring to prominence a new element, namely technical knowledge, organized in the form of a 'technostructure.' Consequently, according to Galbraith, power in 'society at large,' once based on possession of capital, now 'passes' to the technostructure.[14]

Variations on Galbraith's theme have resulted in some fanciful exaggerations. For example: 'Since 1945 spectacular events in science and technology ... have pushed our society across a threshold. The magnitude, interrelations and synergistic effects of the new order of science and technology have made it the dominant fact of our times. Knowledge was always power, but it was not always the central and controlling force in society. Today it is.'[15] The well-known writer Peter Drucker concurs. He describes the most important of all the broad changes now occurring in society as follows: 'Knowledge, during the last few decades, has become the central capital, the cost center, and the crucial resource of the economy. This changes labor forces and work, teaching and learning, and the meaning of knowledge and its politics. But it also raises the problem of the responsibilities of the new men of power, the men of knowledge.'[16]

Caldwell and Drucker stress three subsidiary points: First, knowledge is the greatest economic resource in the modern productive process. Second, the organization of knowledge – defined by Drucker as 'the systematic and purposeful acquisition of information and its systematic application' – is the key to understanding the use of knowledge as a productive force. Third, knowledge must be managed, and therefore development of a capable stratum of administrators (knowledge managers) is the most pressing concern of our society. Caldwell says: 'The task of the knowledge administrator ... is to see, as far as feasible, that all relevant knowledge is brought to bear upon the problems that society needs to solve.'[17]

What of the general population who will be affected by the ministrations of the knowledge managers? Their situation has not been entirely ignored. For example, Zbigniew Brzezinski sees a need for continually retraining the population as a whole, so that individuals will be able to adapt to rapid technological changes. This will be part of a larger process: 'As education becomes both a continuum, and even more application-oriented, its organizational framework will be redesigned to tie it directly to social and political action.'[18] In the interval since these lines were published in 1970, post-secondary education indeed has been given a strong push in this direction.

Of course it is expected that the political consequences resulting from these larger trends will be beneficent. The political scientist Robert E. Lane, writing about 'The Decline of Politics and Ideology in a Knowledgeable Society,' suggests that the social decision-making process is already shaped accordingly: 'The dominant scholarly interpretation of policy-making processes has changed in the direction of emphasizing the greater autonomy of political leaders and legislators: with respect to the role of pressure groups, the power elite, and the electorate. If leaders and other legislators are less bound by the domain of pure politics than we had thought, then they are freer to be guided by the promptings of scientists and findings from the domain of knowledge.' In the United States – the country Lane had in mind – national politics in the 1980s seems to have followed a diametrically opposed tack. As we have seen, the recent theory of intellectual capital stresses the organization of knowledge. This fact is of primary importance for the political ramifications of the new social role of knowledge: a fondness for administrative discretion runs throughout the various formulations of the theory. 'People may have to be told,' Lane remarks, 'not that they are miserable, but that the conditions of their lives are, in some sense, remediable.' Apparently the knowledge managers will not just solve social problems but also will mould the public's idea of what its problems are.[19]

In *The Coming of Post-Industrial Society*, Daniel Bell gives a succinct overview of the themes already presented: 'Broadly speaking, if industrial society is based on machine technology, post-industrial society is shaped by an intellectual technology. And if capital and labor are the major structural features of industrial society, information and knowledge are those of the post-industrial society.' Knowledge replaces machinery and land as the key resource in society; possession of technical skills will be the primary route to power; the making of decisions, located primarily in governmental institutions, will have 'an increasingly technical character'; and gradually 'the entire complex of prestige and status will be rooted in the intellectual and scientific communities.'[20]

This sounds like a preparation for technocracy, full of its pious calls for disinterested experts to take the helm of the ship of state and steer it along a rationally chosen course for the public good. Thus one is relieved to encounter Bell's firm rejection of technocratic illusions. In societies with advanced technologies, traditional institutions and interactive structures are transformed in significant ways; but techniques do not displace politics. Contending passions and interests remain, as Bell correctly insists.

Knowledge and Society

The foregoing discussion shows that the increasing importance of technical knowledge (and its basis in theoretical knowledge) as factors of production in industrial society have long been recognized in political economy.[21] At present we are witnessing some of the accumulating effects of this historical process. As contemporary theorists maintain, the recent quantitative increase in application of technical knowledge to production can be expected to change society. Yet actual and potential social changes have been greatly exaggerated and misleadingly presented by some recent commentators. The ideas of earlier political economists show that such trends had been noted and evaluated for a very long time. From this longer perspective, we can take a calmer view of our choices of destinations.

And *choices* among different possible destinations is the main issue here. Contemporary theory of intellectual capital claims that two general changes follow from the importance of knowledge in production: a decline in the traditional handling of social problems in favor of a technical, 'managerial' approach, and a corresponding achievement of social and political influence by a 'technostructure.' But these are by no means the only, nor the most likely, nor the most desirable outcomes.

For example, the theory envisages a society in which everyone is continually being educated. Surely these people will be able to manage their own lives very well. Will they have to be told, as Lane suggested, that their problems can be solved for them by experts? These questions take us back to Marx's undeveloped notion of the 'general intellect' – which I here elaborate upon.

Contemporary theory neglects another possibility. The modern social function of knowledge lays the basis for a wider scope for ad-ministrative action by knowledge managers, or for a new form of status differential based on technical skills. But widespread diffusion of knowledge, including technical knowledge, may allow many citizens to participate effectively in decision-making on complex issues. At different times both conservative and radical writers have emphasized the great importance of knowledge diffusion.

Some time ago, the conservative economist F.A. Hayek called at-tention to the role of 'unorganized knowledge' – of immediate situa-tions and local circumstances – in the preservation of freedom in society; he added that 'dispersal of knowledge' among the popula-tion as a whole is likewise essential.[22] Writing from a very different perspective, John McDermott concurs: 'For the concentration of effective knowledge of and about American society in several giant organizations can lead to no other result than a substantial decline in the capacity of ordinary Americans to control that society and those organizations.'[23] And with his idiosyncratic blend of conser-vative and radical ingredients in *Tools for Conviviality* and other books, Ivan Illich has sought another way of responding to the authoritarian tendencies in technologically advanced societies.

The notion of the general intellect suggests that the individual's practical understanding of the social and natural world, which is what citizens operate with in their daily lives, can keep pace with the sedimentation of technical knowledge in the productive process. In other words, as our productive system increasingly incorporates a rationalist science of nature, individuals may incorporate the new sources of knowledge in their choices about social and political policies. Growth in productive output could be matched by growth in individuals' capacities to use the new wealth justly and fittingly.

A despotic marriage of knowledge and power in technologically advanced societies is indeed possible, but it is not inevitable. We are not tyrannized by the complex technical knowledge incorporated in our society's administrative structures; we simply expect too much of it. No matter how sophisticated, technical knowledge cannot of itself make our responses to contentious social issues more reasonable or more just. Attainment of that objective should be sought through institutional improvements that permit individuals to make better informed, more careful political decisions. Then more people might wisely apply new knowledge to the just resolution of social issues.

In the so-called information society, individuals control their own destiny with the aid of modern technologies – a principal theme of this book. Before we meet that promise again in chapter 9, however, we must pass some formidable obstacles. Chief among them is the notion that powerful imperatives inherent in the structure of technological progress dictate terms and conditions to us that shape our lives.

3
THE FALSE IMPERATIVES
OF TECHNOLOGY:
IDOLS OF THE THEATRE

The modern conjuncture of capitalism and industrialism laid continuous technological innovation at society's door and required that the social consequences of technological progress be 'managed.' Many observers thought that this might prove an impossible task. As we shall see, the critics of industrialism (discussed in the next chapter) believed that too much of value would be lost in the process because machine-based technologies inevitably must impose their own mode of being (a 'mechanistic' approach) on every aspect of the social world and therefore would drive out whatever was incompatible with it. And the critics of capitalism (discussed in chapter 5) believed that so long as capitalism reigned the type of industrial innovations it promoted would have largely negative effects, perpetuating the domination of the many by the few and imprisoning the population in an 'iron cage' of technological rationality.

Although both sets of critics accused a great variety of institutions and events of being responsible for the evils they detected, modern technologies themselves could not avoid being pinned with a hefty share of the blame, since they had become such prominent actors in human events. More recently, most commentators concentrate on the other side of the coin, namely, the social benefits flowing from an institutional structure dedicated to promoting continuous technological innovation. Yet some authors go further and claim that technologies themselves make demands on us that cannot be (and ought not be) resisted. The most familiar expression of this idea is that modern technologies have their own 'imperatives.'

Promoting Science and Technology

The contention that societies should have official policies dedicated to promoting scientific research and technical innovation was formulated just after the end of the Second World War, which had amply demonstrated the massive destructive capabilities of modern industrial technologies. Proponents of this argument got significant government support for scientific research and development (R&D) placed permanently on the political agenda in Western nations.[1] Debates about technology during this period were carried on in international meetings as well. A symposium sponsored by UNESCO in the early 1950s represented one of the first systematic statements on the social consequences of technological progress, and the contributions made there illustrate many of the approaches that were later pursued in more detail.[2]

By the 1960s, however, substantial concerns about the social effects of technologies had arisen again, and significant collective research efforts were put into place in order to examine those concerns. A learned journal (*Technology and Culture*) devoted to this theme was established, and major projects on technology and society (Harvard University) and on technology and values (University of Pittsburgh) were undertaken. The issues that we shall take up here received a good deal of attention under the heading 'technology and social change,' and a huge bibliography was quickly accumulated.[3]

During this period a few authors worked out an influential conception of the relationship between technology and society. The substantive issues of interpretation arising out of that conception – undoubtedly still widely held – are easily posed. Those whose writings will be examined are R.J. Forbes, Emmanuel G. Mesthene, John Kenneth Galbraith, and Jacques Ellul.[4] Ellul's work appears to be an extremely 'pessimistic' analysis of technology; I will try to show, however, that his basic approach is the same as that of the larger camp of 'optimistic' thinkers.

What is the hallmark of their thought? Its fundamental conception is indicated in a set of familiar phrases: technological order, technical civilization, technological society, technological man, and so on even unto the 'technetronic society.'[5] This terminology implies that modern technologies bring into being a form of society qualitatively different from all previous types; the peculiar dynamic of this technology necessitates far-ranging adjustments in social and individual behaviour. All these writers refer to the imperatives of technology[6] and suggest that we are experiencing a radical discontinuity in human history, a sharp break with the past and the preparation for a far different future.

Their language is often dramatic. Forbes writes: 'Technology can no longer be viewed as only one of many threads that form the texture of our civilization; with a rush, in less than half a century, it has become the prime source of material change and so determines the pattern of the total social fabric.'[7] For Ellul, too, the technological order – the total integration of specialized techniques used in all domains of social endeavour – determines the separate features of society, imposing a uniform mode of organization on the whole. Positive or negative evaluation of this development is, according to Ellul, less important than appreciation of it as a form of social organization different from everything in past human history.[8]

Mesthene's feeling is rather more joyous, but the basic point is similar: 'Technology, in short, has come of age, not merely as a technical capability, but as a social phenomenon. We have the power to create new possibilities, and the will to do so. By creating new possibilities, we give ourselves more choices. With more choices, we have more opportunities. With more opportunities, we can have more freedom, and with more freedom we can be more human. That, I think, is what is new about our age. We are recognizing that our technical prowess literally bursts with the promise of new freedom, enhanced human dignity, and unfettered aspiration.'[9]

The first step in evaluating these notions is to inquire how the key term *technology* is being used. The authors are straightforward in their definitions. Mesthene regards it as 'the organization of knowledge for the achievement of practical purposes.' Galbraith concurs: 'Technology means the systematic application of scientific or other organized knowledge to practical tasks.' Forbes notes the definition offered by Webster's *Third New International Dictionary* ('the science of the application of knowledge to practical purposes'), which appears to be the source for Mesthene and Galbraith, and then formulates his own: 'Technology, then, is the product of interaction between man and environment, based on the wide range of real or imagined needs and desires which guided man in his conquest of Nature.' Ellul distinguishes technique and technology (as I shall do later, for different reasons), chiefly because the latter term misleads us into thinking that the technical phenomenon is only an aspect of society, whereas in reality (for Ellul) it pervades the whole. He finds most acceptable Harold Lasswell's definition of technique – 'the ensemble of practices by which one uses available resources in order to achieve certain valued ends.'[10]

Quite obviously these definitions are rather loose; one can trap myriad types of evidence in such liberally constructed conceptual nets. Stéphane Bernard, who wrote a careful theoretical treatise on the topic, warned against this tendency: assessing the social consequences of technological progress required some reasonable delimitation on the concept of technology. He distinguished loose and restricted senses of the term and suggested use of the restricted sense.[11] Judging from the evidence at hand, his advice went unnoticed.

If modern technology must be seen (according to the authors under review here) as a general social phenomenon, rather than as just the accumulated technical capability of society, then its genesis must be explained. A phrase such as 'the organization of knowledge for practical purposes' begs the questions of who is doing the organizing and to what end. Whence come these 'imperatives' of technology? Alone in this group, Ellul treats this matter most extensively, relating it to a 'change in attitude on the part of the whole civilization.' After asserting that the ultimate reason for this dramatic change escapes us, he lists five factors whose convergence produced the novel technological order.[12] All these factors in turn require explanation, especially the one that Ellul calls the most decisive ('the plasticity of the social milieu'), and, although he recognizes this requirement and attempts briefly to satisfy it, this remains one of the weakest features of his book. The technological order, 'autonomous' and 'self-augmenting,' shrouds its own dynamic and tends to restore an aura of mystery to the workings of society.

For Galbraith the imperatives of technology are related to the structure of the 'industrial system.' This in turn possesses a highly deterministic character: 'It is a part of the vanity of modern man that he can decide the character of his economic system. His area of decision is, in fact, exceedingly small. He could, conceivably, decide whether or not he wishes to have a high level of industrialization. Thereafter the imperatives of organization, technology and planning operate similarly ... on all societies. Given the decision to have modern industry, much of what happens is inevitable and the same.'[13]

The framework for Mesthene's position differs in emphasis but not in substance from that of Ellul and Galbraith. His method is to trace the impact of technology 'on' various facets of social existence, as is shown in the subheadings of one of his essays: 'how technological change impinges on society,' 'how society reacts to technological change,' 'technology's challenge to values,' and so forth.[14] In explaining the process of technological change, he writes: 'I do not depreciate the interaction between technology and society ... Nevertheless, once a new technology is created, it is the impetus for the social and institutional changes that follow it.'

What is responsible for the creation of a new technology? Mesthene tells us that 'the initiative for development of technology in any given instance lies with people, acting individually or as a group, deliberately or in response to such pressures as wars or revolutions.'[15] This can hardly be regarded as an explanation. The entire analysis is designed to trace the immense impact of modern technologies on social behaviour. We are told, in a passage quoted earlier, that 'our technical prowess literally bursts with the promise of new freedom, enhanced human dignity, and unfettered aspiration,' and we are asked to believe that a great flowering of individuality is to be expected therefrom.[16] And all of this is to be attributed to the actions of 'people'! Here social theory dissolves into commonplaces.

Technology and Possibility

Two other interconnected propositions will be found in this literature. First, the chief social function of technology is to create new possibilities for human activity; and, second, in terms of its social effects, technology is 'neutral,' that is, the fruits of technological progress may be used 'for good or evil,' depending on the ends to which they are put. Mesthene states them best: 'Technology ... creates new possibilities for human choice and action, but leaves their disposition uncertain. What its effects will be and what ends it will serve are not inherent in the technology, but depend on what man will do with technology.' And in short form: 'Technology spells only possibility, and is in that respect neutral.' Ellul says: 'But a principal characteristic of technique .. is its refusal to tolerate moral judgments. It is absolutely independent of them and eliminates them from its domain.'[17]

If we compare these remarks with those cited earlier, we encounter a contradiction between the idea of technology itself and the social process of which technology is a part. This technology which 'spells only possibility' seems to be a curiously passive phenomenon, for everything seems to depend on the forces 'outside' technology that determine how it will be used. But the earlier account, stressing the imperatives of technology, gave a very different impression. Another writer's bold formulation of the technological imperative makes the inconsistency clear: 'But, as we are learning, technological innovation belongs to us less than we belong to it. It has demands and effects of its own on the nature and structure of corporations, industries, government-industry relations and the values and norms that make up our idea of ourselves and of progress.'[18] Here technology is not neutral with respect to established values, but rather exerts pressure on them to change in ways that are consistent with its own mode of being.

Technologies cannot simultaneously be neutral and exhibit imperatives and entail positive consequences. If they are really and completely neutral with respect to human purposes, if they involve 'only possibility,' no positive results at all can be attributed to technologies as such. We can go further. According to the neutrality thesis, no determinate ends (either good or bad) can be associated with technologies themselves. Thus, strictly speaking, no consequences at all (and likewise no imperatives) flow from technologies.

This inconsistency shows an enduring problem in our understanding of modern technologies and their social consequences. On the one, historical side we have abundant empirical knowledge about the history of technical innovations, including the conditions of their development and their diffusion within and among different nations. On the other, speculative side, evaluations of the social consequences of technological change remain trapped in the seemingly arbitrary polarization between subjective feelings of pessimism or optimism, and between warnings of doom and complacent advocacy of a 'technological fix.'

In other words, as soon as we move from empirical investigation, concerning such matters as rates of innovation and technology transfer, to general social theory, we encounter extravagant claims about the overall impact of modern technology on social change. Some writers emphasize the beneficent aspects of this process, chiefly the expanding realm of personal choice and individual freedom claimed to flow from technology's achievements. At the other extreme are those like Ellul who see modern technology as a corrosive force that penetrates and undermines the institutions on which society depends.

Both views are fatalistic: they regard social institutions as being forced to adjust to changes brought about by technological innovations and ignore or play down the reciprocal influence that conflicting social interests exert on innovation and application. Neither formulation permits us to reconcile the widely divergent claims about the social significance of modern technologies. Under these circumstances it would not be surprising if some observers were to conclude that the best solution would be to discourage speculative thought on this subject altogether. A less radical therapy involves following up on our close look at the usages of key terms with some suggestions for improvements in terminology.

Definitions

The ideas reviewed above about technology – its imperatives, its autonomy, its involving only possibilities, and its neutrality – have a common fault: they place too much of a load on the concept of technology. To repair it I suggest distinguishing among techniques, technologies, and modes of social reproduction.

Techniques are solutions to practical or theoretical problems arising out of the environmental forces that impinge upon organisms. In plant and animal life, techniques are adaptive responses to environmental forces, and among social animals such responses may be intergenerationally transmitted through learning patterns. Considered as solutions to problems, techniques are mostly the outcome of individual responses and are relevant only to individual settings. Those that transcend such limited settings and become incorporated into the behavioural patterns of social groups represent transmissive solutions and thereby have an evolutionary significance for a particular species. Techniques, considered as operational responses to environmental conditions, are not restricted to human action.

In human societies, techniques encompass all sorts of activities – saving souls as well as manufacturing steel. And here their origination has relative autonomy from their contextual settings, for many technical solutions have lain dormant or been forgotten and subsequently rediscovered, to be used later under much different circumstances. They may result either from random selection, governed by environmental interactions not understood, or from reflective activity and an explicit desire to control the play of environmental forces. Human techniques do not only pertain to the material realm of physical matter and forces but are intrinsically ideational as well.

Those transmissive techniques that attain general significance in particular societies or historical epochs become *technologies*. The main reason for distinguishing between techniques and technologies is that only general modes of social organization, not the specific properties of techniques themselves, determine which types of techniques will be encouraged and promoted and which will be played-down or perhaps forbidden. For example, techniques of magic have been developed and practised in many different cultures, and there is a specific rationality appropriate to them.[19] In some cultures, such techniques have a socially legitimated public function, which may be institutionalized in formal roles and training. In others, such as our own, they may be widely practised in private life but have no legitimate public function. This has nothing to do with the techniques' degree of 'operational perfection' but rather reflects predominant modes of social reproduction and social authority.

The 'rationality' of a culture's selection of techniques should be judged primarily in relation to the socially legitimated goals for individual behaviour in that culture. In this sense it was reasonable for medieval Europe to invest far more individual talent and energy in elaborating techniques of salvation rather than those of material production. The predominant social patterns determine what kinds of techniques will be valued and whether the privileged techniques will remain relatively unchanged or will be continually refined and developed. For example, in many types of what we call primitive society warfare is one of the established, legitimate modes of social reproduction (as a determinant of roles, personal development of individuals, and so forth). The techniques of combat and weaponry are adjusted to the cultural function of ritual warfare, and in most cases of this type they do not change over long periods.

The viability of any culture's behaviour patterns can be judged externally in terms of its comparative reproductive success – its ability to survive and maintain its identity in relation to its competitors. So long as this general requirement is met, we can say that its techniques are appropriate, no matter how bizarre or irrational they may seem from the viewpoint of a different time or culture. In terms of the general ecological form of human societies, hunter-gatherer economies and their associated techniques seemed to possess long-term viability until they succumbed to an alternative pattern involving domestication of plants and animals and development of progressively larger social group units.

The fact that similar techniques have a different significance in various cultures and that the same techniques can have differential social functions at various times in a culture can be reflected conceptually in the distinction between techniques and technologies. This is because the selection and 'weighting' of the operational characteristics represented in a technique both condition and are conditioned by other social factors, such as class, status, and role determinations. The development and use of techniques never occur independently of determinations of who can use them and for what purposes. Such determinations reflect and affect the social division of labour and the tempo of social change.

Technologies, therefore, are combinations of techniques, and the combinations represent choices among alternative uses or goals in the service of which the techniques are applied. In most cases it is inaccurate to refer simply to 'technology,' because very often this term implies some fixed character in a society's technological apparatus. But this is not the case. Rather, there are almost always alternative technologies potentially present in any ensemble of techniques. Certain technologies are 'released' and put into practice, and others are suppressed, by the institutional forms that predominate in any society at a specific time. In themselves techniques are inherently 'abstract:' they set out a solution for a problem involving a relationship between means and ends, and it is a matter of indifference – considering *only* the operational characteristics of the technique itself – who performs the relevant operations and under what conditions.

So far as a society or culture is concerned, however, this is not at all a matter of indifference. In established social patterns, techniques are almost always combined with class, status, and role determinations that specify who can perform the operations associated with techniques and under what culturally legitimated conditions. This combination is what I call a technology, and it is 'concrete' (as opposed to the abstractness of a technique) because it is only in this context that techniques become operational and productive beyond the purely private sphere of existence.

In a culture in which role determinations prohibit women from hunting, a spear is more than the sum of its technical attributes. The same is true of a sword in a society that restricts participation in warfare to the members of a closed social class. Thus every technology has a social character, albeit not a fixed one, incorporating tools or techniques in an operational context that normally will be congruent with the predominant institutional structures and social determinations of a culture. Certainly techniques can be incorporated or combined in a variety of ways in different cultures, and cultures have differential capacities for adopting new techniques and for recombining techniques within alternative technologies.

Just as techniques are incorporated into technologies, so are the latter in turn incorporated into wider frameworks that I call 'modes of social reproduction.' These are the predominant forms of institutional organization in economy, politics, and social relations. The distribution and significance of power, authority, property, class, status relationships, and social roles are the decisive attributes of these institutional forms. The choices made among alternative technologies in any society can be understood only in relation to these attributes.

The dominant modes of social reproduction in modern society, considered as totalities in terms of ideological systems, are capitalism and socialism. As an 'ideal type' or system of ideological principles, capitalism combines such institutional forms as representative democracy, concentration of control over productive resources in privately owned corporations, an economy based on largely unregulated market exchanges, and a minimal public-sector presence. Such a system will have a bias in favour of technologies that enhance the power of these institutional arrangements – for example, industrial technologies that concentrate the labour force into large units under managerial control and that can produce goods with market prices that will assure adequate corporate profits.

As this system has evolved into one of managed capitalism during the twentieth century, the role of government as ultimate regulator of the economy has expanded. At the same time, the general standard of living has risen dramatically, giving the whole population a permanent material stake in how the economy functions. This new type of quasi-market political economy has a strong bias in favour of industrial technologies that can deliver a never-ending variety of consumer goods.[20]

In countries that espouse official socialist ideologies, the dominant institutional forms are authoritarian political systems, 'command economies' with highly centralized economic planning, a labour force in which almost everyone in effect works for the state, and a small sphere for private market exchanges. For the most part this system has favoured industrial technologies that maintain the rigid control of a centralized bureaucracy which combines political and economic authority. A distinctive characteristic of this system is the production of consumer goods with notoriously poor quality, because the technologies of production are strictly subordinated to the overriding need to maintain authoritarian-bureaucratic domination.

There is now abundant evidence that the system of authoritarian socialism is breaking down, largely because it is incapable of delivering an acceptable standard of living for the populations under its control. This means the end of centralized economic planning, far wider scope for autonomous action by production units, the end of guaranteed employment security, and in general the spread of market-oriented decision-making throughout the economy. Technologies of production must be altered accordingly; for example, producers will have to be able to ascertain changing patterns of consumer behaviour and to redesign their wares in response to mutations in tastes and fashions.

Technological Hyperbole

Strictly speaking, there are no imperatives in technology. The chief mistake made by the writers examined above is to isolate one aspect (technology) of a dense network of social interactions, to consider it in abstraction from all the rest, and then to relate it back to that network as an allegedly independent actor. Whether we are interested in contemporary times, or in earlier societies – as the historian Lynn White Jr has been – the lesson is the same: the significance of technical innovations in human societies is an integral part of the whole cultural matrix.[21]

In the conceptual scheme proposed here, technology stands as the middle term between techniques and modes of social reproduction; indeed, technologies may be thought of as the synthesis of the other two. Practical and operational aspects stemming from technical innovations present an abstract capacity for action in the world; prevailing modes of social reproduction in a given society determine *who* can act and in what ways. For example, among the Siane people of the New Guinea highlands, contact with Europeans prompted transition from stone to steel axes; however, in that culture only men use axes, and this gender and role differentiation determined the social uses of changing axe technologies there.[22]

Thus technologies may be thought of as 'embedded' techniques – as operational capacities necessarily interlaced with the prevailing institutional forms in a social system. There are no imperatives in technology itself, because the synthesis that it represents is indeterminate and unstable. The synthesis is indeterminate because the way in which techniques are combined with different aspects of different social and cultural systems – not the operational characteristic of techniques themselves – constitutes the impact of a technology. And the synthesis is unstable because most social systems are constantly evolving not rigidly unchanging entities. Thus both the significance and the impact of a technology in a given setting can change over time.

What I call technological hyperbole is the systematic and unwarranted exaggeration of the effects of the purely technical aspects of technologies 'on' social systems. The fruits of such hyperbole are ideas such as the imperatives of technology, which give us the impression that we must adapt our ways to the requirements of the instruments we have devised or suffer adverse consequences of one sort or another.

Although it often appears as if we are being subjected to the pressures of the technological imperative, something quite different is actually occurring. To understand what it is, we need only return to our starting point – Francis Bacon's program. For Bacon, as we have seen, technological progress represented our great hope of an escape from society's traditional zero-sum games, where gains and losses cancel each other. Since Bacon's time modern societies have adopted the strategy of using the continuous advance in technical innovation as the path of least resistance in their striving to maintain social peace; in other words, they have learned to resist reallocative demands (the zero-sum game of shifting resources from one social class to another) by holding out the promise of increased wealth for everyone. New technologies are the key to increasing the total economic product. The 'price' we must pay for this service is to accommodate the patterns of everyday life to the organizational requirements of those technologies (the factory system, massive white-collar bureaucracies, specialization of functions, regular replacement of one set of skills by another, and so on). But it only appears as if the technologies 'cause' these transformations. In fact the driving force behind the changes is and always has been the larger social strategy indicated above, to which the dominant institutions have harnessed the boundless energies of technical innovation.

From the standpoint adopted here, which sees technologies as mixtures of techniques and social responses, the pressures of the technological imperative appear a misperception; we over-emphasize the characteristics of techniques and undervalue the dynamic aspects of the societal matrix in which they are used. But when we glance again, in the next chapter, at some of the most famous nineteenth-century literary works, and re-experience the sense of foreboding that was attached then to industrial technology, we will understand better the peculiar and enduring force of this misperception.

4

SUBLIME MACHINE:
IDOLS OF THE MARKET-PLACE

The show-stealing exhibit at the Philadelphia Centennial Exposition in 1876 was a Corliss steam-engine, weighing 680 tons and standing thirty-nine feet high, which provided all the power for the entries in Machinery Hall. According to contemporary accounts, its presence overwhelmed all who entered the hall, whether they were ordinary fair-goers, such high and mighty as President Ulysses S. Grant and the emperor of Brazil, or well-known writers like William Dean Howells. It excited the popular imagination, as had other such events beginning with the Great Exhibition in 1851, and so outstripped the capacity of ordinary descriptive reporting that only ecstatic metaphorical construction could register reactions to it. John F. Kasson notes that the fair-goers' descriptions of their experience 'frequently became incipient narratives in which, like some mythological creature, the Corliss engine was endowed with life and all its movements construed as gestures. The machine emerged as a kind of fabulous automaton – part animal, part machine, part god.'[1]

One guidebook for the Philadelphia exposition offered its readers a lesson in aesthetic judgment. Whereas traditionally poets located the experience of the sublime in our reactions to wild nature or powerful human passions, the guidebook claimed that the modern age recognized the sublime in the design and operation of its great machines. And a newspaper reported that in the presence of the Corliss engine 'strong men were moved to tears of joy.'

Almost exactly one hundred years later the French 'neo-Dadaist' artist Jean Tinguely persuaded the director of New York's Museum of Modern Art to offer the museum's sculpture garden as the site for a spectacular auto-da-fé by Tinguely's self-destroying machine. (The performance was named *Homage to New York*.) When finished, the machine was twenty-three feet long and twenty-seven feet high; its main distinguishable components were a piano, an old Addressograph machine, eighty bicycle wheels, steel tubing, a meteorological balloon, a huge klaxon on wheels, a wide assortment of small mechanized devices, and various chemicals – smoke, flash powders, and foul-smelling substances.

When the main motor was switched on, the piano keys were struck, wheels turned, klaxons sounded, a radio blared, clouds of smoke billowed forth; a number of small constructions broke free and wheeled about; and small objects were hurled through the air. Then the piano caught fire, the steel tubing supports began to give way, and the terrified museum authorities ordered in firemen with axes and extinguishers to finish off the machine. Once set in motion, the machine's self-destructive orgy had followed pretty much its own course, rather than the artist's specific sequence of events, and this spontaneity was precisely what Tinguely had hoped most to achieve. To him this machine 'was the opposite of the skyscrapers, the opposite of the Pyramids, the opposite of the fixed, petrified work of art, and thus the best solution he had yet found to the problem of making something that would be as free, as ephemeral, and as vulnerable as life itself.' The late machine was described as both a beautiful and a terrible thing, and it was reported that at the end some spectators had wept.[2]

All in all the concept of the sublime – the ineffable union of awe and dread, terror and attraction – is as good a guide as any to unravelling the modern reaction to industrial society and the machine. The iconography of the machine supports the case. Kasson remarks that many nineteenth-century popular illustrated magazines chose a graphic style and accompanying text for their drawings of large machinery that heightened the sense of 'mystery and majesty.' One of the most famous illustrations was J.O. Davidson's *Interior of a Southern Cotton Press at Night* (1883). Davidson himself supplied the following explanatory note: 'Beneath the converging rays of electronic lamps and reflectors a most weird effect is produced, for the machine assumes the aspect of a grand and solemn demon face, strangely human, recalling the famed genii of the Arabian Nights.'[3] In the great scene in Fritz Lang's film *Metropolis* (1926), where tier upon tier of identical machines, deep underground, are attended by workers whose rhythmic movements follow those of the levers and dials, the machine's face closely resembles the one engraved by Davidson.

The iconic representation of the machine, in eliciting the feeling of the sublime, testified to the darker side of the human experience with large-scale machinery that qualified the popular enthusiasms expressed at the great exhibitions. This popular ambivalence was mirrored in the struggles by imaginative writers and social thinkers to come to terms with the industrial age.

The majority of nineteenth-century political economists, and virtually all the marginalist economists who created a formalized discipline after them, typified the 'happy consciousness' of industrial society; they were satisfied that the abundant and manifest benefits supplied by industrialism and the division of labour overawed whatever negative aspects inevitably accompanied them. They never entirely silenced the dissenting voices, however, who worried about the moral degeneration and degradation of skills in the labour force. Originating in a striking passage in Adam Smith's *Wealth of Nations* (1776), this dissenting strain was kept alive mainly in the nineteenth-century socialist movement, notably by Robert Owen, Karl Marx, and William Morris. It remains alive in the twentieth-century tradition that runs from Thorstein Veblen to Ivan Illich.

Many dissenting social thinkers believed, however, that the degeneration characteristic of industrial society was remediable, in most cases by more or less drastic reordering of economic and political circumstances. It was much different with those who represented the predominant aesthetic sensibility of their time, for among them the prevalent mood ranged from dismay to horror. Beginning about 1830, when the impact of industrialism began to register, major writers entered the lists against the machine and the industrial age: Thoreau, the later Emerson, Melville, and Henry Adams in the United States; Zola, Balzac, and Flaubert in France; Heine, Hesse, and Thomas Mann in Germany; in nineteenth-century England, Carlyle, Dickens, Ruskin, and Morris, and in the early twentieth century, Forster, Lawrence, and Huxley.[4] For some of these it is (at least overtly) a minor theme, but for others the machine becomes the symbol of degeneracy itself. This mood's culminating expression is the great anti-utopian novel of the early twentieth century, Yevgeny Zamyatin's *We*.

The anti-industrial sentiment also predominated in major English and European developments in the plastic and decorative arts, in part as a reaction against the influence of industrial design on public works and consumer goods. The Aesthetic Movement and Art nouveau set their faces resolutely against mechanical reproduction and industrial design. Only in the 1920s did architecture and design begin to reconcile themselves to the industrial age.

One can date the aesthetic reaction to the machine from 1829, when Thomas Carlyle's great essay 'Signs of the Times' baptized his period the 'Age of Machinery.' This reaction is completed almost exactly a century later, with the publication of the two greatest anti-utopian novels, *We* (written in Russian in 1920, but published first in English translation in 1923) and *Brave New World* (1932). George Orwell was the first to identify Zamyatin's theme: 'What Zamyatin seems to be aiming at is not any particular country but the implied aims of industrial civilization ... It is in effect a study of the Machine, the genie that man has thoughtlessly let out of its bottle and cannot put back again.'[5] An allusion to the genie, which we have already encountered in J.O. Davidson's commentary on his illustration of the cotton press, is itself one of the most common textual threads in the literary response to the machine age.

The aesthetic response to industrialism after 1830 argued the shallowness of other reactions, especially in political economy and social thought. The latter were, as suggested above, divided into a predominant 'happy consciousness,' which welcomed industrialization with open arms, and a dissenting minority, which wanted urgent institutional changes to counteract its deleterious impact on labour and social relations. Most of those in the latter category, however, contended that these negative aspects could be overcome and that the machine age could be turned unambiguously to mankind's benefit.

The dominant literary metaphors appeared to rule out this eventuality. For at its deepest level the matter appeared to be one of life and death, considered in terms of the essential determinants of what it means to be human, and the machine seemed to represent the ultimate degeneration, the death of humanity. In the following pages this theme will be tracked through a series of metaphorical constructions that lead inexorably to the opposition of life and death.

Root Metaphors

Sander L. Gilman has used the idea of 'root-metaphor' as a way of understanding both continuities and variations over time in literary expressions that reflect common experiences.[6] It seems that we often require a means of synthesizing our perceptions of complex events, especially when we are faced with startling new circumstances that fall outside the realm of our ordinary experience. Metaphors – 'it was like a thunderclap' – allow us to capture a novel or extraordinary event in forms of thought that are well known to us, thus 'domesticating' it; furthermore, they encourage us to believe that we may communicate our experience to others. There is a concomitant risk, of course: metaphorical constructs limit our ability to assimilate new information, because we try to squeeze the unusual into familiar and comfortable form.

That established ways of life are challenged by unremitting technological novelty is something of a cliché for us by now. Yet we who have become so jaded should not forget how profoundly unsettling was the sprouting of large-scale machinery and the factory system for both society and culture in the nineteenth century. For most people, common folk and artists alike, it was as if the world itself had come unhinged. Many found that they could comprehend its significance only by resorting to metaphorical expressions rooted in thoroughly familiar structures of experience. When one recalls the enormity of the changes wreaked in the social and physical landscape in such a relatively short time, it is unsurprising that the search for adequate expressive modes should terminate in the fundament itself: life against death.

No simple scheme can hope to capture all the varieties of expression for such a universally felt experience. The one to be explored here seems to catch a sample of reasonable size and quality, although undoubtedly much that is equally important slips through its mesh. The scheme is composed of three levels of metaphorical construction, internally related to one another, which proceed from the 'surface' realm of familiar social experience to the ultimate duality of life and death.

The root metaphor for the surface level of representations of the relationship between humanity and the machine is *master and servant*. This had two quite obvious advantages. First, it was a relation that was thoroughly familiar in social experience everywhere. Second, and perhaps most important, it is a relation that is readily reversible in imagination. The affirmative response to industrialism trumpeted the machine as the perfect servant of human objectives, as the long-sought deliverance from necessity and want. The rejoinder quickly made itself heard: the servant will be master. The imagery of the 'sorcerer's apprentice', together with that of the Arabian Nights and its genii, have been favoured to make this point.

The root metaphor for the second level is further development of the master-and-servant theme. Domination and servitude are external relations in which each side is necessarily the opposite of the other. At the seond level we pass beyond this purely external relation, and the two participants in the human-machine relation begin to switch roles: human agents adopt more passive roles in step with the growing virtuosity of machinery. Machinery based on advanced designs is capable of self-regulation and self-adjustment; at the same time the human agents who tend the machines have less and less to do. There arises the twin prospect of the autonomy of the machine and people as automatons. The second level of representation is therefore *autonomy/automaton*.

The 'autonomous technology' theme is an old and persistent one in Western thought.[7] Conceiving the machine as autonomous is an extension of the master-and-servant metaphor. At the second level the machine's role in the relation is reversed – servant is now master – in the sense that we have allowed ourselves to become utterly dependent on its productive power in providing desired goods; strictly speaking, then, this is a case of voluntary servitude. In other words, we set in motion a course of events that resulted at some point in our losing control over what we have created: we can no longer 'freely' choose to have it or not. Since we cannot even conceive of doing without its benefits any more, we are beholden to our apparatus, and we begin to adjust our behaviour to its modus operandi. In Carlyle's words: 'Men are grown mechanical in head and in heart, as well as in hand.'

What began as an external relation is now an internalized process, whereby the dependent member (the human being) surrenders its own authentic being to its erstwhile instrument. The relation itself and the tension between its originally opposed sides dissolve as human society begins to mimic the way machines operate. In *We* Zamyatin gave the most striking representation to the process of internalization and the root metaphor of autonomy/automaton: society is ordered on the model of the machine, and men and women are its subordinate parts, whose 'functions' are determined strictly in relation to their role in the apparatus as a whole.

The third level of root metaphor was a direct outcome of what preceded it: the concept of automaton led directly to the imagery of the opposition between life and death. This metaphor works on the identification of the machine with inorganic matter, necessity, repetition, and identity, and thus death – and the concomitant association of life with organic processes, and with contingency, variation, or freedom. The machine as automaton, however, possesses characteristics both animate and inorganic; in crossing over the two realms it appears to draw what is living inexorably into the province of the inanimate. Powerful representations of this theme appear in the case studies to be presented later: Melville's 'The Paradise of Bachelors and the Tartarus of Maids,' E.M. Forster's 'The Machine Stops,' and Zamyatin's *We*.

Machinery

For industrialism's defenders, machinery had lifted a double yoke from humanity's shoulders, namely, subjection to nature's capriciousness as well as to the corrupting influence spread by relations of dependence among people. Technology would overturn humanity's age-old subordination to physical forces and deliver the realm of nature holus-bolus into its hands, to do with as it would. At the same time, material abundance and mechanical aids would do away with the employment of people in personal service – an especially prominent theme in the United States, where industrialism had been linked to republicanism. Two years after Carlyle's 1829 essay appeared, its message was thoroughly rejected by a writer for the *North American Review*, Timothy Walker, in 'Defence of Mechanical Philosophy.' Of the blessings of technology he wrote: 'From a ministering servant to matter, mind has become the powerful lord of matter.'[8]

This Baconian theme, both widely sown and deeply rooted by mid-century, was so successful in its propagation because it represented the relation between human beings and large-scale machine technology as analogous with the completely familiar routine of masters and servants. Machines would take the place of servants, who are out of place in a democratic regime; not only could it assume many of the burdensome tasks usually imposed on dependent people, and in many cases perform them more efficiently, but it could also be seen to be more fitting in this role. John Ruskin gave a nice explanation for this point. What a master ordinarily requires of his servants, he remarked, is the maximum output for the least pay (that is, the market value of the servant's labour); and, according to the prevailing economic wisdom, this situation will yield the greatest benefits for society as a whole and all its individual members, including the class of servants.

This would be the case, Ruskin objected, 'if the servant were an engine of which the motive power was steam, magnetism, gravitation, or any other agent of calculable force'. On the contrary, the servant is a human agent whose 'motive power is the Soul,' and this fact marks an essential difference: 'The largest quantity of work will not be done by this curious engine for pay, or under pressure, or by the help of any kind of fuel which may be supplied by the cauldron. It will be done only when the motive force ... is brought to its greatest strength by its own proper fuel: namely by the affections.'[9]

Ruskin's distinction reinforces the metaphor of the master-servant relation as a way of understanding the machine's significance for human life, for always lurking in this relation is the potential reversibility of its terms. Thus the machine can be seen as replacing the human agent and as doing the bidding of human masters. But much folklore also tells of the 'reversal of fortune' that catapults erstwhile servants into their master's place to lord it over those who formerly had abused them. Just so the machine.

Melville used the notion of a reversal of roles between humanity and machinery in his portrayal of a New England paper mill in his short story 'The Paradise of Bachelors and the Tartarus of Maids' (1855): 'Machinery – that vaunted slave of humanity – here stood menially served by human beings, who served mutely and cringingly as the slave serves the Sultan. The girls did not so much seem accessory wheels to the general machinery as mere cogs to the wheels.'[10] This was to become a favourite image in the critique of industrial society, especially in the utopian literature that argued for a 'second reversal,' to be achieved by radical reordering of social relations to re-establish humanity's hegemony over the instruments to which it had become enslaved. In his utopian sketch *A Traveler from Altruria* (1894), William Dean Howells suggested this in a way that reinforced the root metaphor; in his imaginary future society, 'the machines that were once the workman's enemies and masters are now their friends and servants.'[11]

The resolution proposed in 're-reversal' confines the relation between humanity and machinery to the first level of root metaphors.

It finds adequate the representation given by the metaphor: machines should be regarded as our servants. And it identified our problem as solely one of re-establishing our right to occupy the dominant side in this relation. As we shall see, this seemed a rather superficial resolution to those who wished to consider the matter in terms of deeper levels of significance and more profound root metaphors. For the re-reversal slips too readily over the circumstances that had given rise to the original reversal, that is, the one whereby human agents had become the machine's servants.

The change in Ralph Waldo Emerson's attitude over a period of twenty years offers a clue about these circumstances. He began with robust confidence in the industrial age and its possibilities for improving the human condition: the enormously influential essay 'Nature' (1836) trumpets that nature 'is made to serve.' Illustrating what Leo Marx calls Emerson's 'rhetoric of the technological sublime' is the following 1843 entry from his journal: 'Machinery and Transcendentalism agree well.'[12] *English Traits* (1856) records a different sentiment, however: 'But a man must keep an eye on his servants, if he would not have them rule him ... It is found that the machine unmans the user. What he gains in making cloth, he loses in general power ... The incessant repetition of the same hand-work dwarfs the man, robs him of his strength, wit and versatility, to make a pin-polisher, a buckle-maker, or any other specialty ... Then society is admonished of the mischief of the division of labour, and that the best political economy is care and culture of men.'[13]

Industrialization

Emerson's mention of pin-polishing stands in ironic contrast to the famous opening chapter of Adam Smith's *Wealth of Nations*, which had heaped praise on the division of labour and had made Smith's own pin-making illustration a legend in the subsequent political economy literature.

Seventeenth-century Europeans were unable to decide whether the barbarous ways of the New World inhabitants were a degenerate form of earlier civilized conditions or simply a case of arrested development.[14] Their successors may not have resolved this point, but they were confident at least that they knew the proximate cause of their misery: according to Adam Smith, the 'savage nations of hunters and fishers ... are so miserably poor' because their labour productivity is so low, and this in turn results from their ignorance of the benefits bestowed by the division of labour.

Smith also knew how to reckon the price paid for economic progress, however. The mental faculties of everyone in 'barbarous societies' remain 'acute and comprehensive' and are not 'suffered to fall into that drowsy stupidity, which, in a civilized society, seems to benumb the understanding of almost all the inferior ranks of people.' The division of labour confines the ordinary worker's activities to routine tasks: 'The man whose life is spent in performing a few simple operations ... has no occasion to exert his understanding ... He naturally loses, therefore, the habit of such exertion, and generally becomes as stupid and ignorant as it is possible for a human creature to become ... His dexterity at his own particular trade seems, in this manner, to be acquired at the expense of his intellectual, social, and martial virtues.' Material progress is won at the expense of widespread degeneration in mental faculties and the capacity for exercising good judgment in public and private affairs.[15]

The Tory critique of industrial society inspired by Carlyle made much of this theme, claiming that the proponents of industrialism and economic development regarded the working population as nothing but 'animated machines.'[16] Their opposition lent voice in the political arena to the widespread anti-machinery sentiment among the working classes in the early phases of the factory system and to the tremendous social disruptions that accompanied it. The Tory critique's force diminished as it became increasingly apparent that the necessary concomitant to its attack on industrialism was preservation of a traditional agrarian economy and social hierarchy. This left sustained opposition effectively in the hands of the radical critics, who also objected to the degradation of labour and skills under industrialism, but who steadfastly maintained that under radically different social arrangements the highest possible degree of application of machinery to production was in the workers' interests.

Among all who were willing to commit themselves to this course, Marx grasped best its profoundest implications: 'In no way does the machine appear as the individual worker's means of labour ... Not as with the instrument, which the worker animates and makes into his organ with his skill and strength, and whose handling therefore depends on his virtuosity. Rather, it is the machine which possesses skill and strength in place of the worker, is itself the virtuoso, with a soul of its own in the mechanical laws acting through it ... The science which compels the inanimate links of the machinery, by their construction, to act purposefully, as an automaton, does not exist in the worker's consciousness, but rather acts upon him through the machine as an alien power, as the power of the machine itself ... The production process has ceased to be a labour process in the sense of a process dominated by labour as its governing unity.' The labourer ceases to be the 'chief actor' in the production process and becomes instead only the 'watchman and regulator' over it.[17]

The radical tradition split into two quite different currents in response to the growing presence of machinery in production and the consequent deskilling of labour. The most influential current, in which Marx and most modern socialists are found, accepted the declining role of labour and its traditional skills in producing life's necessities and relegated the cultivation of skill and virtuosity to the realm of 'free time' or leisure. A much smaller branch, for which William Morris's utopian tract *News from Nowhere* (1890) is the chief source, drew the opposite conclusion: re-establish skilled craft labour as the cornerstone of social life and limit wants and satisfactions to what such effort can provide with the smallest possible reliance on mechanical assistance.

The factory system methodically undermined labour's autonomy, its very 'substance' as an agent in social life, by eliminating society's dependence on the rich panoply of craft skills heretofore distributed among the working classes. The historical residue of those skills is absorbed by the system of machinery, 'whose unity' – in Marx's striking formulation – 'exists not in the living workers, but rather in the living (active) machinery, which confronts their individual, insignificant doings as a mighty organism.' In this light it is easy to see why the master-and-servant metaphor, so readily applied to the relation between humanity and machinery, was also so readily reversible. Having appropriated the essential substance of its putative master, the machine was heir to humanity's accumulated, alienated mastery of its environment; what remained for the 'stupid and ignorant' mass of deskilled labourers was only numbing exhaustion in the service of the machine's imperious rhythm.

The radical critique maintained that the machine could be remastered and compelled once again to serve mankind's purposes. The system of machinery confronts the worker as an automaton or as a 'living, mighty organism' at the level of immediate experience; labour is cowed into submission because it appears as if all skill, initiative, and 'virtuosity' have passed irrevocably from it to another kind of being. Its apparent otherness and autonomy, however, upon analysis turn out to be just that, mere appearance. In truth it is the same substance: machinery is 'objectified labour,' the material legacy of past human skill and exertion, misappropriated in the form of privately owned capital. What seemed to be service to the machine was in fact subjection to another human group that had discovered in large-scale machinery a wondrous device for extracting vast wealth from the labour of others. The realization that labour's enemy was not the machine but the capitalist was for the radical critique the 'beginning of wisdom' and the first step toward re-establishing labour's autonomy.

An implicit rejoinder to this program was made in the period under review, governed at the second level by the root metaphor of autonomy/automaton: specifically, internalization of the machine principle in humanity's own mode of being. From this perspective, labour's wresting of control of the industrial system away from the capitalists would be Pyrrhic, for this would seal the fate of society as a whole, committed irrevocably to mechanistic modes of action. The very moment of its triumph simultaneously would signal labour's final defeat, and its ostensible autonomy would be a sham. Labour and its skills would be no longer the heart of the production process, since it had surrendered that role to machinery; labour – or what was left of it, namely, superintendence – would become just a routine social obligation to earn income for consumption.

In accepting machine production as the dominant means for supplying life's necessities, modern society would be forced as well to adopt a mechanistically oriented routine for life in general: 'The relation in which the consumer, the common man, stands to the mechanical routine of life at large is of much the same nature as that in which the modern skilled workman stands to that detail machine process into which he is dovetailed in the industrial system. To take effectual advantage of what is offered as the wheels of routine go round, in the way of work and play, livelihood and recreation, he must know by facile habituation what is going on and how and in what quantities and at what price and where and when, and for the best effect he must adapt his movements with skilled exactitude and a cool mechanical insight to the nicely balanced moving equilibrium of the mechanical processes engaged. To live – not to say at ease – under the exigencies of this machine-made routine requires a measure of consistent training in the mechanical apprehension of things.'[18] These comments by Veblen in his *The Instinct of Workmanship* (1914) were not meant to encourage any hope that this 'machine-like process of living' could be overturned. The best one could do was to take it to its logical conclusion by placing engineers instead of businessmen in charge.

When this concern was first raised, almost a century earlier, it was possible to surmise that the swelling tide of mechanization might yet recede again. The great manifesto for those who so believed was Thomas Carlyle's 'Signs of the Times' (1829). For Carlyle the physical instruments rapidly overtaking traditional productive processes were only the visible expressions of a deeper malaise, namely a habit of mind and action he described in precisely the same terms as Veblen would use much later: a pervasive 'matter of factness.' The machine itself served as a metaphor for 'the great art of adapting means to ends ... by rule and calculated contrivance.'[19]

Carlyle begins his animadversions by referring to the transformations in the physical environment wrought by the application of machinery to production and transportation. Besides its obvious effects in undermining the craftsman's position, mechanization is faulted for being unable to distinguish between appropriate and trivial applications. By these means people seek to rule nature and in doing so pay a heavy price: 'Not the external and physical alone is now managed by machinery, but the internal and spiritual also.' Here the machine stands for the disappearance of spontaneity and for the rise of a mode of action that first appraises each situation in strategic terms, then breaks down ultimate objectives into a manageable series of discrete steps, and then assigns means from whatever quarter to the separate tasks: 'Has any man, or any society of men, a truth to speak, a piece of spiritual work to do; they can nowise proceed at once and with the mere natural organs, but must first call a public meeting, appoint committees, issue prospectives, eat a public dinner; in a word, construct or borrow machinery, wherewith to speak it and do it.'[20]

By the time he came to write *English Traits* (1856), Emerson had lost his youthful enthusiasm for the industrial age and was ready to echo Carlyle's sentiments: 'Mines, forges, mills, breweries, railroads, steam-pump, steam-plough, drill of regiments, drill of police, rule of court and shop-rule have operated to give a mechanical regularity to all the habit and action of man. A terrible machine has possessed itself of the ground, the air, the men and women, and hardly even thought is free.'[21] Taken as a metaphorical allusion, the last sentence could do nicely as an epigraph for E.M. Forster's story 'The Machine Stops.'

Neither Carlyle nor Emerson, however, was yet prepared to concede that all was lost. There was still time to reverse this disastrous course and to reassert the pre-eminence of the natural and the spontaneous over the mechanical mode of action. Despite its deepening penetration of public and private life, mechanization was not yet triumphant over the old ways. Carlyle advertised this hope in an especially revealing way, namely, by suggesting at the end of his essay that the fundamental root metaphor governing the first level of representation was still operative: 'Indications we do see in other countries and in our own, signs infinitely cheering to us, that Mechanism is not always to be our hard taskmaster, but one day to be our pliant, all-ministering servant.'[22]

This curious conclusion by Carlyle seriously undermines the force of the argument that preceded it. For it suggests that, however widely it had spread, mechanism had not contaminated the original sources of human action and still could be subordinated to individual and collective ends governed by non-mechanical principles. Or perhaps the opposite is nearer the mark: the force of his own earlier argument undermines Carlyle's conclusion.

Automatons

Matching the uninterrupted march of machine technology in the second half of the nineteenth century was a growing fear that it was indeed out of control. In the relation between humanity and machines, increasingly the former seemed to be the passive partner and the latter the active agent. The more the system of machinery as a whole assumed labour's erstwhile attributes – skill and indeed virtuosity (Marx) – the more the worker appeared 'like a machine' in the derogatory sense, fit only for the dull repetitiveness of routine operations. Emile Zola, who on other occasions rhapsodized about modern technology, filled his Rougon-Macquart novels with allusions to the machine-like and thing-like character of human action and, correspondingly, with the appearance of animate force and autonomous power residing in machinery.[23]

As early as his writings of 1857–8 Marx had referred to an

'automatic system of machinery' as the 'most complete' and 'most adequate' form of the machine itself, 'set in motion by an automaton, a moving power that moves itself; this automaton consisting of numerous mechanical and intellectual organs, so that the workers themselves are cast merely as its conscious linkages.'[24] The root metaphor of autonomy/automaton, which was to be fleshed out as a favourite device in fiction, alluded not so much to a reversal of roles, as in the case of the master/servant metaphor, as to a complete collapsing of the two sides of a relation into a synthetic entity that transcended both. Its most effective representation was the man-like automaton.

Herman Melville's story 'The Bell-Tower' (1855) is thought to be the first fully developed portrayal of such a creature.[25] The story is headed by Melville with an anonymous epigraph, the third passage of which reads: 'Seeking to conquer a larger liberty, man but extends the empire of necessity.' In the story itself, a 'great mechanician,' Bannadonna, is commissioned to construct a huge belltower; after the tower itself has been completed, he insists on working in secrecy on the belfry, eventually having a large object, concealed in wrapping, hauled up. Bannadonna alone remained in the belfry when the day came to inaugurate the ringing; the entire population waited below, but at the appointed hour, instead of the anticipated booming of the great bell, only a single muffled sound was heard, followed by silence.

Upon entering the belfry the town magistrates found the dead Bannadonna and standing over him an enormous mechanical figure, cast by its creator to run upon a track at each appointed hour and strike the bell with its arms. Bannadonna, intent on some finishing touches to the bell, had forgotten the hour and had been struck dead by the mechanical figure.

Yet, according to the story's narrator, this was to have been only the prototype for Bannadonna's ultimate creation, an 'elephantine helot' to be produced in great numbers and incorporating all the characteristics of all the animals that mankind had heretofore yoked to its will: 'All excellences of all God-made creatures, which served man, were here to receive advancement, and then to be combined in one.' And the figure itself was to epitomize the aesthetics of the sublime: Bannadonna's design principle for it was 'the more terrible to behold, the better.'

Bannadonna had intended to give his 'metallic agent' not only the power of locomotion but also 'the appearance, at least, of intelligence and will.' The terror inspired by the physical appearance of the automaton has its source in a deeper dread, originating in its violation of the border between life and death: inorganic matter, becoming animate by a process of purely mechanical or chemical operations, inevitably produces a reverse effect and draws the living into the realm of the dead. This is the third and final level of root metaphors about the machine.

In 'The Paradise of Bachelors and the Tartarus of Maids' (also 1855), Melville casts the relation between humanity and machinery in these terms. The story's unusual structure is especially interesting, for Melville portrays the degeneracy or sterility of machine-based civilization not by contrasting it to a healthier, unmechanized condition but rather by juxtaposing it to another kind of sterility represented by traditional culture. The result, while wholly negative in tone, seems to make the point forcefully that there is no succour there.

The 'Paradise of Bachelors' section recounts a long and very alcoholic dinner enjoyed by an old group of bachelors in an elegant private club in London; the story then shifts without transition to the 'Tartarus of Maids' section, which describes a paper-mill factory in New England that employs a work-force made up only of young women. Both are based on visits by Melville, the first at Elm Court in Lincoln's Inn in 1849 and the second at Pittsfield, Massachusetts, in 1851.[26]

The 'Paradise of Bachelors' is a scene of sedate, well-tempered pleasure. The meal itself, although consisting of many courses, is curiously undistinguished fare; the dominant imagery is of the bachelors' carefully modulated consumption style: not a one sneezes when the snuff is passed around. The meal itself is, as Dillingham remarks, 'a metaphor for their orderly existence.' The impression of sterility and lifelessness is transmitted both by their dispassionate overindulgence in food and drink and by the state of lifelong bachelorhood to which all are committed.

The whole story's structure – the abrupt succession of the two sections – employs the first as backdrop for the second. The intrinsically powerful imagery of sterility and death in the second section is heightened further by being presented against what had preceded it. The latter section is saturated with such imagery: the narrator-traveller's close brush with death, the pallor in the female workers' faces, the blankness of the paper, the factory ('like some great whited sepulchre'), the setting: 'The mountains stood pinned in shrouds – a pass of Alpine corpses.' The traveller sees the apparatus inside the factory: 'Something of awe now stole over me, as I gazed upon this inflexible iron animal. Always, more or less, machinery of this ponderous, elaborate sort strikes, in some moods, strange dread into the human heart, as some living, panting Behemoth might. But what made the thing I saw so specially terrible to me was the metallic necessity, the unbudging fatality which governed it.'

It is not just that the machine is the living entity; procreative allusions indicate that it has assumed the generative capacities of life as well. The machine is housed in a room that is 'stifling with a strange, blood-like, abdominal heat'; and the elapsed time between the introduction of the pulp and the emergence of the finished paper is 'nine minutes to a second.' The female workers are all unmarried virgins whose very substance drains away. In the finished paper the traveller sees 'glued to the pallid incipience of the pulp, the yet more pallid faces of all the pallid girls I had eyed that heavy day.'

The reference to the 'necessity' and 'fatality' of the machine reinforces the epigraph to 'The Bell-Tower': there is no escape from necessity through machine technology; on the contrary, that way leads to greater bondage.

One can assume that for Melville the world outside the machine's orbit was still vibrant and that no irreversible commitment to it had been made. By the end of the nineteenth century it seemed to many that such a commitment indeed had been extracted from a society seemingly enthralled by the system of machinery, especially in North America. The dominant opinion seemed to be that whatever unease the machine might evoke paled into insignificance beside the more immediate dangers against which man and machine warred side by side: the power of untamed nature, wilderness, and the surviving remnants of savage cultures. There is a marvellous representation of this attitude in the Currier and Ives lithograph *Across the Continent* (1868).[27] A train is drawn up before a rough frontier settlement, on the other side of which two mounted native warriors stand; the train itself is the protective hedge for civilization against the as-yet-untamed wilderness.

Early-twentieth-century imaginative fiction recognized this complete commitment (or capitulation) to the machine. The external form of representation that characterizes the first and second levels of root metaphors – the machine confronting mankind as master/servant or as automaton – gave way to imagery of full internalization. Portrayed in its most striking terms, the man/machine symbiosis emerged fully developed, with the inevitable result: degeneration of the physiological and psychological autonomy of the human agent. The machine appeared as metaphor for a human society organized as a single, machine-like organism.

E.M. Forster described his story 'The Machine Stops' as 'a counterblast to one of the heavens by H.G. Wells.'[28] The human population resides underground, living singly in compartments where, at the pressing of buttons, mechanical devices supply water, food, air, beds, medicine, music, and communicating devices. Travel outside the compartments, although provided for, becomes rare, with a resultant deterioration in skin and musculature. Vashti, the central character, is described as a 'swaddled lump of flesh,' with 'a face as white as fungus.' Originally the interlocking, supportive mechanism that sustains life in the compartments had been directly superintended by its designers; as their dependence became habitual, however, the human agents seemed to lose control over the functioning of the apparatus, which also had been supplied by its inventors with self-repairing mechanical aids. Soon they began to pray to it. That was the beginning of the end: 'But humanity, in its desire for comfort, had overreached itself. It had exploited the riches of nature too far. Quietly and complacently, it was sinking into decadence, and progress had come to mean the progress of the Machine.'

Eventually the mechanism collapses, taking with it the compartmentalized inhabitants. But they were already dead in all but name, the living dead. Kuno, Vashti's son, had tried to explain this to her before the end: 'Cannot you see ... that it is we who are dying, and that down here the only thing that really lives is the Machine? We created the Machine, to do our will, but we cannot make it do our will now. It has robbed us of the sense of space and the sense of touch, it has blurred every human relation and narrowed down love to a carnal act, it has paralyzed our bodies and our wills, and now it compels us to worship it. The Machine develops – but not on our lines. The Machine proceeds – but not to our goal. We only exist as the blood corpuscles that course through its arteries, and if it could work without us it would let us die.'

Hope for regeneration lies only in the rude bands of escapees or natives who exist completely outside the orbit of mechanized society. This theme recurs in *We* and *Brave New World*.

In *We*, the individuals – who carry such designations as D-503 and I-330 – are described as the 'cells' of the 'single mighty organism' that is the One State. All live in identical rooms and are nourished by a single, industrially produced substance. The Table of Hours regulates all movements, setting prescribed times for eating, work, exercise, and sleep, except for the two Personal Hours each day – which, it is expected, will soon become part of the 'general formula' like the others. Zamyatin's imagery is dominated throughout by mathematical allusions. According to the sexual law, for example, each 'number' (individual) is entitled to have sexual relations with any other: 'You declared that on your sexual days you wish to use number so-and-so, and you receive your book of coupons (pink). And that is all. Clearly, this leaves no possible reasons for envy; the denominator of the happiness fraction is reduced to zero, and the fraction is transformed into a magnificent infinity.'[29]

Society itself is the machine, an organism of differentiated and smoothly integrated component parts. A mechanism in the usual sense, the physical object, appears in *We* only as a symbol: first, as the Integral, a spaceship designed to bring the message of 'mathematically infallible happiness,' achieved in the One State, to other planets; and, second, as the Benefactor's Machine, a device to cauterize the area of the brain that houses the faculty of imagination. The *One State Gazette* announces to the citizenry: 'Until this day, your own creations – machines – were more perfect than you ... The beauty of mechanism is its rhythm – as steady and precise as that of a pendulum. But you, nurtured from earliest infancy on the Taylor system – have you not become pendulum-precise? Except for one thing: Machines have no imagination ... The latest discovery of State science is the location of the center of the imagination: a miserable little nodule in the brain of the pons Varolii. Triple-x-ray cautery of this nodule – and you are cured of imagination – forever. You are perfect. You are machinelike.'[30]

As the novel ends, D-503, chief mathematician for the Integral project, submits voluntarily to the operation: 'It is the same as killing myself – but perhaps this is the only way to resurrection. For only what is killed can be resurrected.' Once the operation is universally performed, and the imaginative faculty is genetically blocked in future generations, the mechanism itself will be needed no longer: society-as-machine will have removed all remaining impediments to its smooth functioning and will be able to reproduce itself identically for all time to come. But, at the city's edge, there is chaos, as the remnants of older humanity assault the surrounding Wall.

The matter-of-factness that Veblen identified as the behavioural orientation of the machine age has today become the expected routine of everyday life. We are accustomed to quantitative measure in every aspect of social relations. The calculation of benefits and costs in numerical terms pervades our lives – in negotiations between prospective marriage partners as well as between unions and corporations, in setting minimum levels of welfare payments as well as maximum 'throwweights' for nuclear missiles. Domestic life is unimaginable anymore without mechanical devices, and more and more people carry around inside their bodies some testimony to the wizardry of medical technology.

As well, an abundance of automatons in all sorts of horror films and science-fiction literature during the last fifty years has inured us to them; the ubiquitous video games should dissolve whatever remains of the machine's threatening visage. A few scattered souls may still quake at the prospect of self-programming computers becoming obstreperous, or of chess grandmasters being humiliated by an unanswerable gambit from a machine opponent, but for most the terror and dread, as well as the sublimity, that fired the nineteenth-century mind are gone. The relation between mind and machine is now grist for esoteric philosophical debate in the academic mills; the combat in this zone, however fierce it may become, is unlikely to revive that older mood.[31]

The master of the new style is the Polish writer Stanisław Lem, and the mode of representation is whimsy. *Mortal Engines* introduces us to 'electroknights' and 'ultradragons' and to a computer that calls itself 'Digital Grand Vizier' and insists on being addressed as 'Your Ferromagneticity.'[32] *The Cyberiad* opens with a story about a machine that suffers with good grace the ridiculous commands of its inventor, although it cannot resist a touch of spite. The stories are infinitely comforting, because Lem's machines have all the pathetic emotions and foibles so readily recognizable as our own. And, after all, Jean Tinguely's self-destructive machine was designed to show precisely that the machine shares with us life's essential attribute, namely mortality, and is thus an affirmation of life rather than its negation.

5
THINGS IN THE SADDLE: IDOLS OF THE CAVE

In the preceding chapter, reference was made to a remarkable passage in Marx's work, where he foresaw one of the truly revolutionary aspects of industrialism. Once complex machinery was in regular use everywhere, he guessed, the process of production would cease to be under the direct control of human agents and instead thereafter would be mediated by a technological apparatus of ever-growing size and complexity: 'In no way does the machine appear as the individual worker's means of labour ... Not as with the instrument which the worker animates and makes into his organ with his skill and strength, and whose handling therefore depends on his virtuosity. Rather, it is the machine which possesses skill and strength in place of the worker, is itself the virtuoso, with a soul of its own in the mechanical laws acting through it ... The science which compels the inanimate links of the machinery, by their construction, to act purposefully, as an automaton, does not exist in the worker's consciousness, but as an alien power, as the power of the machine itself ... The production process has ceased to be a labour process in the sense of a process dominated by labour as its governing unity.' In other words, a radical inversion occurs. Where formerly human labour was the centre-point of the production process, and tools assisted in realizing labour's tasks, now – in the experience of most workers – mechanized technologies would stand at the centre, and labour thereafter would be their servants.

Certainly Marx realized that this inversion produced a huge leap in society's ability to create material wealth: he opened *Capital* with an observation to this effect. It is well known that Marx and his followers also held that, under the capitalist form of industrial development, the majority of people were deprived of their rightful share of this new wealth, and further that they believed that they knew how to remedy this defect. It is less well known that Marx, as well as some of the most talented theorists among his followers, introduced a stubborn inconsistency into the radical theory of social change, through their reflections on this technological apparatus of production.

On the one hand, they claimed that an exploited social class could seize control of this apparatus – both the accumulated technological infrastructure and the goods produced thereby – and turn this apparatus to its own advantage. On the other hand, they continued to refer to a peculiar quality inherent in the apparatus itself, something 'mysterious' or 'apparently autonomous' or 'resistant' to being commanded to serve a different set of human purposes. Like the nineteenth-century writers discussed in chapter 4, they found something obdurate in the machine and its fruits.

Marx labelled this something the 'fetishism of commodities'; Lukács renamed it 'reification'; Sartre called it the 'practico-inert'; and Marcuse, 'instrumental rationality.' Emerson's famous lines from 1847 capture the idea: 'Things are in the saddle, / And ride mankind.'

The Fetishism of Commodities

Marx's reading notes from his student days show his keen interest in primitive religion, especially in fetishism in African societies.[1] The terms *fetish* and *fetishism* are Portuguese in origin, and they were coined in accounts of fifteenth-century European voyages of discovery to Africa. In Edward Tylor's analysis of this literature, a thing is a fetish-object when it is thought that a spirit is embodied in it or is acting or communicating through it.[2]

Marx did not at first make much of this notion. One would expect it to have been given prominence, especially in his *Economic and Philosophical Manuscripts of 1844*, where he presents a dramatic image of the product of human labour that subsists as a 'hostile' object vis-à-vis its creator. But the *Manuscripts* were written under the spell of Hegel's terminology, especially the concepts of estrangement (Entfremdung) and alienation (Entäusserung), and Marx uses the term *fetishism* only in passing, with reference to money.

Before writing the famous section on the fetishism of commodities at the end of chapter 1 in the first volume of *Capital*, Marx used the term rarely and casually.[3] For most of the late 1840s and the 1850s he was preoccupied with either polemical tracts or journalism and was reading widely in the history of political economy. In the late 1850s, when he turned to offering a systematic account of the nature of capitalist society, he was at some point reminded of the notion of fetishism. I think that the way in which he thought about capitalism and about how he would present this systematic account of it brought back this notion from the depths of memory.

Following Hegel's method, Marx claimed that one must begin at the level of appearances, that is, how the phenomenon being studied (capitalism) 'showed itself' to the observer. It did so predominantly as a world of goods or commodities. He opened his first published study of commodity production, *Contribution to the Critique of Political Economy* (1859), with a statement to this effect, which he used again to open *Capital* eight years later: 'The wealth of societies in which the capitalist mode of production prevails appears as an immense heap of goods [ungeheure Warensammlung].'[4]

An immense heap of goods, or, as the phrase is usually rendered, immense collection of commodities: a vast world of things. From there Marx plunged straight into his dissection of the essential nature of the commodity, using the categories of use-value and exchange-value that were conventions in political economy but seeking to extract a great deal more meaning from them than others had. Only in the last short section of that extraordinary opening chapter does the basic point emerge. However, chapter 2 moves in different directions, and 'the fetishism of commodities' is not taken up again, and much of its potential impact was lost.

As a social system, capitalism represents itself as an ever-expanding world of goods, attributing its success to allowing market mechanisms free play in the economy. According to Marx, something is missing or hidden. Another phenomenon, of no lesser significance than the world of goods itself, is overlooked or suppressed, leaving a great lacuna in our experience of social relations. What was missing or hidden was adequate representation of the human commonality of effort in the economic activities of 'production' and 'consumption.'

The conventional ideology of the market-place, which concentrates on decisions by individuals about buying and selling (including the selling of their labour power), failed to give any sense of collective social meaning to all this frenetic activity. For the industrial society of Marx's day this was no mere debating point, since individuals were being drawn out of tightly knit rural communities, where social networks based on personal associations were omnipresent, into the looming anonymity of urban environments. Some other basis of social unity was indeed being created, but it had not been recognized as such and thus could not be acted on; according to Marx, this missing representation was the growing social character of the labour process.

What was missing, therefore, was an awareness that 'socialized labour' created capitalist wealth. Above all else, capitalism required the ability to construct a national (and ultimately international) division of labour, forcing people out of permanent local or regional attachments, creating great aggregations of different types (male, female, children) and skills, so that changing labour-force requirements could meet with rapid response. By such means, the distribution and development of factory training among the working population could yield optimum productivity for the national economy as a whole. Much later there would arise the widespread recognition that all persons can benefit (albeit unequally) from rising labour productivity, providing a strong foundation for a common interest in economic progress. But not yet.

For Marx the social character of labour – the ensemble of factory skills being combined with the new technologies to revolutionize the production process – was the real source of the continuing growth in the wealth of capitalist society. But it was not represented or recognized as such. Instead, an abstract force known as 'the market' was seen as responsible for this revolutionary transformation in creating material wealth. According to Marx this was paradoxical: the creation of wealth through labour, the most fundamental form of human action, was said to be driven by an impersonal mechanism that was not under the direct control of human agents. The instrument of wealth-creation (the market mechanism or generalized commodity production) was seen as a kind of living force in human affairs. And this meant that there was inevitably a mysterious or mystical element inherent in market-place goods.

Marx called the use-value of goods the 'matter' or material element in commodities: the characteristics that make things useful for satisfying human needs of all sorts. Exchange-value is their 'form': a type of value (usually represented in a thing's money price) that will enable us to compare its worth to that of other things. He saw no mystery about whether particular things were or were not useful, since everyone could tell whether something satisfied a need or not: 'The mystical character of the commodity does not therefore arise from its use-value ... Whence, then, arises the enigmatic character of the product of labour, as soon as it assumes the form of a commodity? Clearly it arises from this form itself ... The mysterious character of the commodity-form consists therefore simply in the fact that the commodity reflects the social characteristics of man's own labour as objective characteristics of the products of labour themselves, as the socio-natural properties of these things ...; the products of labour become commodities, sensuous things which are at the same time suprasensible or social.'[5]

Marx's language is provocative: a few paragraphs further on he speaks of 'the whole mystery of commodities, all the magic and necromancy that surrounds the products of labour on the basis of commodity production.' What exactly is he referring to? In generalized commodity production based on an advanced division of labour, most people work at creating only one part of a single product (say, the pulping process in a paper factory), and then they will seek to satisfy their needs by purchasing a variety of finished products (food, clothing, entertainment, and so forth) that they had no hand in creating. Unlike the conditions where handicraft labour prevails, where all stages in the creation of most things are likely to be familiar to both those who produce them and those who consume them, market-industrial production 'hides' the concrete relations between the qualities of finished goods and the particular human skills that made them.

Thus paper products for consumers emanating from industrialized production, for example, are generally more abundant, versatile, varied in texture and appearance, and durable than are handcrafted papers; in other words, their qualities give rise to a far wider range of uses. Most people who use the final products do not know which particular human skills and technologies (which are themselves just accumulated past skills) were responsible for creating those qualities. When we, as consumers in the market-place, encounter such products, their qualities appear to us as the inherent aspects of the things themselves. This is, I think, what Marx means when he says that the social characteristics of labour appear as the 'natural' properties of produced things themselves. And, given the astonishing capacity of industrialism to turn out new types and qualities of things, it can be said that there is something magical and mysterious about all this.

Marx goes on to say that the commodity-form 'is nothing but the definite social relation between men themselves which assumes here, for them, the fantastic form of a relation between things.'[6] He gives an analogy, saying that this is just like religious systems, which project what are really human creative powers onto non-human entities (gods, angels, devils, and so forth), which then seem to act autonomously, as if they had 'a life of their own.' In like manner the unrestricted play of market forces makes it seem as if material things have a life of their own: they and their qualities appear and disappear, their prices (and thus access to them) move in no apparent relation to urgent human needs, and at times of economic recession or depression the whole system of objects collapses inexplicably, bringing widespread destitution and misery.

Of course Marx's main point was that there is nothing really mysterious going on here. Decisions by actual human agents, the owners of capital, not allegedly impersonal market forces, are responsible for what happens in the world of goods. But was the general population duped by the apparent mystery? He had spoken of magic and mysticism, and of misleading appearances, but not about the consequences possibly flowing therefrom. To be sure, the analogy with religion recalls the expression 'opiate of the people,' but the mysteries of commodity production do not seem to be an arena of especially comforting illusions, as Marx thought religion was. Rather, we may be closer here to the idea of 'false consciousness' (although Marx never used the term), and it is not unreasonable to suppose that Marx was thinking along these lines, even though he did not even suggest that the population as a whole might be infected with such a malady as a result of commodity fetishism.

If Marx made so little of the fetishism of commodities, as is certainly the case, why should we not regard it as just a theoretical curiosity? Suitably transformed and elaborated, this notion became a cornerstone of twentieth-century Western Marxism. In those later versions both the vast world of things and the ever 'denser' apparatus of industrial technology associated with them took on great significance for the theory of radical social change. In fact these phenomena became the chief explanation for the failure of the mass revolutionary consciousness to arise; in the end, their brooding presence in Marxist theory is remarkably similar in tone and content to the sentiments we have already witnessed coming from many nineteenth-century writers.

Reification

Lukács's concept of reification is nothing less than an intellectual tour de force, a deft amalgamation of materials from Marxist doctrine with the writings of his contemporaries Georg Simmel and Max Weber. His bold thesis, stated at the outset of his essay 'Reification and the Consciousness of the Proletariat' (1922), was that the 'problem of commodities' should be seen as the main issue in the fate of capitalist society.[7] In taking this step, he transformed a theoretical curiosity (Marx's fetishism of commodities) into a full-blown theory of social consciousness and the predicted breakdown of capitalism. This conception also became the single most significant influence on the subsequent history of Western Marxism, including the writings of the Frankfurt School. I intend to deal only with a single aspect of Lukács's essay – the notion of a world of things that appears to have a 'life of its own.'

Marx had illustrated his concept of fetishism by contrasting what he thought were 'typical' economic relations in the medieval and modern periods. According to Marx, in medieval times economic relations were largely services and payments 'in kind.' They took the form of contractual obligations, such as what was owed by a serf to the lord of the manor, which were fulfilled directly by supplying goods (such as grain) and labour services (work on the lord's fields), rather than by paying the monetary equivalents of the value of those things. In the modern period, all such obligations and exchanges are converted into a monetary form. Marx concluded that in medieval times 'the social relations between individuals in the performance of their labour appear at all events as their own personal relations,' whereas in modern times social relations are 'disguised as social relations between things, between the products of labour.'[8]

The contrast itself is reasonably clear. When, at the end of the growing season, a serf handed over to the manorial lord whose land he tilled half of his crop, a crop that he and his immediate family had tended, presumably it was plain that the social relation – the legally enforceable obligation standing behind such transactions between all those who happened to fall into the categories of 'serf' and 'lord' – was also a 'personal' relation, in the sense that each party presumably knew who the other was. In a modern market society, the labour activities of actual people are rendered anonymous in the production of things: we do not know who made the things we use. Since in purchasing things for consumption we can find no trace of the identities of those who made them, it could be said that here things wear a kind of disguise, showing no trace of the personal interactions that occurred during their production, exchange, and use.

Marx did not draw any specific conclusions about the likely consequences of the two situations he contrasted. Thus the reader is left with the question: 'So what?' Furthermore, it is difficult to see what conclusions he might have drawn. For during the latter half of the nineteenth century, say, when struggles between workers and capitalists were often bitter and violent, whatever 'disguise' Marx had in mind did not prevent most workers from identifying their adversaries as distinct persons – 'the bosses.' There was very little doubt about who the 'other' was in the endless crusade to win better wages and working conditions and to reduce the arbitrary power of the factory owners. What was in doubt, as Marx knew very well, was whether the crusade's objectives should be limited to those just mentioned or carried on to a 'final' revolutionary conclusion in the dispossession of the owners.

Lukács took his inspiration from Marx's contrast and reformulated it so that it had a general application: 'The separation of the producer from his means of production, the dissolution and destruction of all natural production units, etc., and all the social and economic presuppositions necessary for the emergence of modern capitalism tend to replace natural or original relations [urwüchsige Beziehungen], which exhibit human relations more plainly, by rationally reified relations.'[9]

The 'separation of the producer from his means of production' occurs when most people work for wages in settings where raw materials and production facilities are privately owned by a relatively small group. Producers (workers) are separated from the things needed for production (raw materials, tools and machinery, etc.): owners may decide arbitrarily to deny access to them unless their terms for wages and other matters are agreed to. In such settings, labour-power is a commodity within an economic form in which all or most of the goods that satisfy human needs are also commodities. How do people in this situation regard the sphere of economic activity?

According to Lukács, the 'objective side' of this situation – how the domain of work and the satisfaction of needs look to human agents – is represented by the market-place. Here access to goods required for the satisfaction of needs is said to be governed not by a specific group of people but rather by the so-called laws of the market-place, which thus appear independent or autonomous with respect to human will. The 'subjective side' – how human agents regard their own powers and capacities – is estrangement, or alienation: the circumstances that dictate how people can exercise their own abilities and energies are clearly not under their control but seem rather to be set by apparently autonomous market rules.

The passage quoted above shows that Lukács's basic contention about the situation just described is grounded in a contrast between 'natural' or 'original' relations and 'reified' relations. What are 'natural relations'? Lukács was not as clear on this point as he should have been, given its importance to his argument. He indicates indirectly that natural social relations encompass human labour as an 'organic' process that also has an 'organic unity'; further, this process is based in a specific type of setting – a 'village community.' The 'unity' of the goods that labourers produce is also described by him as being 'irrational' and qualitatively determined; as use-values such products have an immediate, qualitative, and material character. Finally, Lukács mentions – apparently as a model that synthesizes this list of terms – handicraft production and the 'organic manufacture of whole products based on the traditional amalgam of empirical experience.' In a moment we shall return to these expressions.

What are reified relations? Here Lukács's descriptive terms are an applied version of Max Weber's well-known concept of formal rationality.[10] Under industrialism, conditions of human labour undergo a process of rationalization with the following characteristics: specialization of function for jobs, mechanization wherever possible, calculation based on quantified units of measure (time and motion studies), and breaking down of productive units into component units (subassembly). Further, we can observe determination of work by units of time (hourly rates), formal equivalence of these quantitative measures across all types of work (comparison of jobs by wage levels), and reduction of qualitative differences in work environments to general industrial averages. Finally, there is fragmentation of the subject of this process (the worker, whose specialized functions are never related evidently to the whole finished product) and in general assimilation of human agents into the whole industrial process as if they were just other mechanical parts of a vast apparatus.

The opposition between these two kinds of relations is nicely epitomized in Lukács's statement that 'the mechanical disintegration of the process of production into its components destroys those bonds that had bound individuals to a community in the days when production was still organic.'[11]

When one synthesizes Lukács's scattered comments, the contrast emerges as quite straightforward. Non-reified (natural or original) relations exist in small communities made up of skilled persons, each of whom independently produces finished articles from ready-to-hand materials, including foodstuffs. Since these are described as 'personal' relations, we must assume that most transactions, whether carried out by direct barter or by some common medium of exchange, are local ones. Working conditions in such a setting differ in every respect from those that obtain under modern, reified relations. Conditions of labour are determined by those who do the work; labour is 'holistic' and 'organic' in that all stages in producing an article are carried through by the same skilled person; labour has an 'immediate' relation to its own product; labour is primarily 'qualitative' in that individual specificity is always imprinted on its products. Finally, the materiality of use-value – the obvious character of the needs that these products are intended to satisfy – stands on an equal footing with whatever formal procedures are devised in order to facilitate economic transactions among persons.

When Lukács grafted the senses of Weber's formal rationality onto Marx's concept of commodity fetishism, the negative connotations carried by each notion reinforced each other. Thus all the composite qualities of reified relations in the labour process are things clearly to be shunned if possible: under these circumstances the labour process is fragmented, mechanistic, and ruled by purely abstract and quantitative determinants. However, all the qualities of original or natural social relations – organic, immediate, holistic – appear to be good things which we should seek to recover.

Quite obviously this will not do as the basis of a theory of social action in modern times, nor even as a theory of socialism. In following what Simmel had called the 'hollow communistic instincts' in the socialist tradition, Lukács was responding to only one side of the duality identified by Simmel: 'Undoubtedly, socialism is directed towards a rationalization of life, towards control of life's chance and unique elements by the law-like regularities and calculations of reason. At the same time, socialism has affinities with the hollow communistic instincts that, as a residue of times long past, still lie in the remote corners of the soul ... The distinguishing features of its power of attraction lie in rationalism as well as a reaction to rationalism.'[12]

In early modern history capitalism had blended the first generalized market economy with industrialism. This blend contained intrinsic features of capitalism (such as control over the means of production by a class of owners), of a market economy (such as wage labour), and of industrialism (such as the factory system). Marx and other socialist theorists announced that society could have industrialism without capitalism, and (in communism but not in socialism) without a market economy as well. Lukács appeared to go further and to promise a socialist or communist utopia that would be spared the 'rationalism' that was for most other observers an essential feature of industrialism itself. But in this version the theory is a farrago, and the expectation of apocalyptic transformation merely a concession to dramatic form.

In a practical sense, of course, nothing came of Lukács's speculative scheme; its significance lay only in its powerful impact on an influential tradition of twentieth-century European thought. It is not generally understood how paradoxical this impact was, however. Lukács's concept of reification presented the fearsome obstacles standing in the way of any emergent 'revolutionary' social consciousness – obstacles far more extensive, more deeply rooted, and more difficult to overcome than any previously identified in the Marxist tradition! Lukács's account, taken to its logical conclusion, would be a definitive analysis of why any expectation of revolutionary change in advanced capitalist societies was totally unfounded.

Without realizing it, Lukács had sketched, in the concept of reification, a compelling image of an autonomously generated world of things, a sphere of objects whose 'laws of movement' were severed from any grounding in the original or natural form of human labour. Each successive step in industrialization pushed the natural condition of human labour further into the past; each such step fastened the iron cage of rationalization and reification more securely about humanity. Toward the end of his essay, Lukács warned that with each passing day the structure of reification 'was sinking more deeply into the consciousness of the proletariat.'[13] At the same time he awarded the proletariat the honour of smashing that false world. The heroic deed failed to occur, but the image remained. It resurfaced in some of the Frankfurt School's work.

Technological Rationality

Marcuse's concept of technological rationality, the center-piece of his best-known book, *One-Dimensional Man*, follows closely Lukács's portrait of reification. He first outlined this concept in a 1941 essay and based it on a contrast between it and what he called 'individual rationality.' The latter was the foundation for modern liberalism and rested on the premise that individuals are or can be autonomous agents, whose thought and action stem from self-reflection and enlightened self-interest, which take place in economic action occurring in free markets as well as in other spheres of life.

But the increasing concentration of economic power in capitalist societies betrayed those hopes, for 'the process of commodity production undermined the economic basis on which individualistic rationality was built,' and this rationality was 'transformed into technological rationality.' In other words, sometime around 1900 the dominant economic units of production (corporations) gradually assumed effective control over operations of the market-place, and thereafter small entrepreneurs lived at the mercy of the great corporations. Henceforth the rationalism that was applied to the task of increasing industrial productivity (Weber's formal rationality) would be embodied in the activities of large organizations. Under these circumstances most individuals would have little choice but to discover how best to adapt themselves to working successfully within large organizational structures, thus bringing their behaviour into conformity with the 'rationality of the apparatus.'

The predominant image conveyed by Marcuse is the absorption of rational techniques by the institutions that steer society – in modern times, the alliance between government and large corporations – which leaves individuals without any 'reasonable' basis for opposing the injustices these institutions perpetrate: 'Individuals are stripped of their individuality, not by external compulsion, but by the very rationality under which they live ... The point is that today the apparatus to which the individual is to adjust and adapt himself is so rational that individual protest and liberation appear not only as hopeless but as utterly irrational.'[13] There results the union of rationality and domination, forged by modern organizations through their command over the tempo of technological progress.

In 1964 *One-Dimensional Man* powerfully restated these themes, calling up a 'technological universe' characterized by a mode of activity that 'shapes the entire universe of discourse and action, intellectual and material culture.' Technology is presented as the key to what is happening in advanced industrial societies, for it is not just a collection of new devices but rather something with an inner unity. What Marcuse calls the 'technical apparatus of production and distribution' functions as a 'system which determines *a priori* the product of the apparatus as well as the operations of servicing and extending it. In this society, the productive apparatus tends to become totalitarian to the extent to which it determines not only the socially needed occupations, skills, and attitudes, but also individual needs and aspirations ... Technology serves to institute new, more effective, and more pleasant forms of social control and social cohesion.'[14] Having painted such a vision, Marcuse found himself in the same predicament as Lukács had: if this is the way things are, how could the promised revolutionary deliverance be forthcoming?

No good answer was given, for the simple reason that none could be. If this technological rationality – reification under another name – was functioning as described, there was no escape. This had to be the unavoidable conclusion to the arguments advanced by both Lukács and Marcuse, yet this last step could not be taken by anyone committed, as they were, to belief in the inevitability of radical social transformation. So the belief persisted irrationally alongside its own refutation, namely, the image of a world of things that had slipped out from under human control and then had returned to dictate terms to its erstwhile creators.

The Practico-Inert

Much of Sartre's *Critique of Dialectical Reason* is directed implicitly against Lukács. This book attempts to give a better account of how the material dimension of existence – what Marx called the 'exchange' between humanity and nature through labour – is incorporated within a dialectical process leading to freedom. According to Sartre, a defensible concept of freedom must address the question of how a natural being, subject to the strict necessity inherent in the physical laws of the universe, can understand its own history as a project, that is, as the struggle to realize self-chosen ends. Sartre suggests that this can be done only by accepting materiality as a constitutive moment in human development, which gives rise to a permanent state of tension between our embeddedness in the domain of the practico-inert and our potentiality for transcending it.

Inertia is one of the chief characteristics of inorganic matter. The element of necessity inherent in our encounter with it lies in the fact that we must deal with it on its own terms and thus affirm ourselves as material beings. Only by exerting physical energy, for example, can we effect desired transformations in nature. And in so doing, human action itself ('praxis') is externalized and embedded in matter: 'In transcending his material condition man objectifies himself in matter through labour.' This is explained more fully in the following passage: 'The meaning of human labour is that man is reduced to inorganic materiality in order to act materially on matter and to change his material life. Through transubstantiation, the project inscribed by our bodies in a thing takes on the substantial characteristics of the thing without altogether losing its original qualities. It thus possesses an inert future within which we have to determine our own future. The future comes to man through things in so far as it previously came to things through man.'[15]

I understand this to mean that all action on the material world is an act of determination that opens certain possibilities and simultaneously forecloses other possible options. This is the 'inert future' in objects that comes to us through them: having invested our energies in devising ways to work with matter (wood, metals, and so forth) in order to create objects that will satisfy human needs, as well as to create the cultural practices that attach symbolic significance to objects, we then must recoup these investments. We do so by arranging the lives of successive generations in accordance with the forms of satisfaction made possible by those objects and practices. Example are religious traditions and their sacred paraphernalia, arts and crafts, and of course technologies.

Although we have determined the form and substance of these objects, they exert a reciprocal determination on us, which may be called the domination over humans by 'worked matter.' This is an inescapable condition imposed on us by our existence as natural beings, the fact that man is obliged to 'objectify himself in a milieu which is not his own, and to treat an inorganic totality as his own objective reality.' Here again we hear the refrain of an earlier theme, much varied in expression but still recognizable, of the human encounter with a world of things that comes to have a 'life of its own.'

Two quite general and rather abstract propositions have been advanced so far. First, humans are obliged to respond to the pressure of their needs by engaging the material world on its own terms, recognizing its 'inertia,' thus acting under conditions not freely chosen by themselves. Second, in doing so they enlarge the immediate presence of the practico-inert domain that surrounds them, and this accumulated 'shell' represents a set of constraints on the range of future action and thus on the realm of freedom. Sartre never adequately discusses his thesis in concrete terms, but he gives some examples of the practico-inert: machines, tools, and consumer goods. He comments: 'These human objects are worthy of attention in the human world, for it is there that they attain their practico-inert stature; that is to say, they lie heavy on our destiny because of the contradiction which opposes praxis (the labour which made them and the labour which utilizes them) and inertia, within them.'[16]

The practico-inert is 'worked matter,' the result of mixing both human labour and human purposes with the materiality of nature. As the sphere of accumulated worked matter grows and becomes more lasting, especially in the development of civilizations and at an accelerating rates with the appearance of industrialism, a paradox emerges. The realm of actual and potential freedom expands as the so-called realm of necessity shrinks, that is, as industrialized societies are better able to provide for life's necessities with a steadily diminishing amount of labour time. But this achievement exacts a heavy price, namely, that people must adapt their behaviour to the demands of the machines that underwrite their deliverance. For example, agriculture, which is the traditional core of labour activity in civilization, must be mechanized and converted into an adjunct of the chemical laboratory; new skills required by innovative technologies must be mastered; and generally a high level of government supervision must be accepted so that potential health and environmental risks associated with new technologies can be managed.

Sartre leaves us with what we might call the 'weight' of history, or more specifically the 'pressure' exerted on us by the world of accumulated things. He undermines the naïve view that sees every step in material progress as simply the arrival at another, higher plateau in human freedom. This view overlooks what Sartre calls the inertia in the dense layers of worked matter within which we have insulated ourselves against the conditions that prevail in natural environments. This dense material substrate of a civilized existence indeed affords us relief from life's necessities, as well as some luxury in varied measure to boot. But our dependence on it also compels us to service that domain of worked matter both directly (by keeping things in good working order) and indirectly (by enlarging the equally dense structures of bureaucratic organization in which most people now labour).

According to Sartre, the weight of the practico-inert tends to unify human actions into social totalities (traditions, institutions) that reflect not freely determined choices but rather the passive inertia of materiality itself. These are essentially passive totalities because they exert strong pressures on individuals to conform to behavioural rules inherited from past conditions. When the lives of social groups are determined by external forces in this way, rather than by their own consciously formulated objectives, humanity subsists in a state of 'being-outside-itself.' To the extent to which traditions and institutions succeed in exacting this conformity, they thus assume, paradoxically, the guise of active forces defining and moulding the lives of individuals. Sartre gives his exposition a dramatic conclusion: as being-outside-itself, humanity is defined as 'bewitched matter' (matière ensorcelée).[17] And this provocative expression nicely brings us back full circle to where we started, when we encountered Marx's puzzling reference to the 'magic and necromancy' that he thought was inherent in commodity production. And also back to the different images of an automaton that Marx and Melville had projected in the 1850s!

Reconsiderations

On the basis of Sartre's conception of the world of things we can now go back and revise the other notions reviewed in this chapter. We can amend Marx's ideas of fetishism and alien power, for example. The sphere of the practico-inert, which includes everything produced under the impulse of human need, always has a 'life of its own' considered in relation to newly emergent, spontaneous expressions of human purposes. Recall Marx's formulation: under conditions of general commodity production 'the products of men's hands ... appear as autonomous figures endowed with life of their own, which enter into relations both with each other and with the human race.' For Sartre this is the mediation of humans by things; what Marx had

postulated as a distinctive feature of capitalist commodity production is actually a universal characteristic of human activity in the
world.

Marx's argument depends on a specious contrast between capitalist
and pre-capitalist economic formations, suggesting as it does that
economic relations in the latter allegedly had an intrinsically 'personal' character lacking in a market-oriented system. If we ignore this
element, there is still something interesting left. Fetishism – the apparent autonomy of things – is a disguise according to Marx: relations
among people are disguised as relations among things. If we now
combine this proposition with Sartre's perspective, fetishism can
be regarded as the phenomenal form of the practico-inert. In 'showing' itself to us, the produced world of objects presents itself as opportunities for our self-realization. At the same time, however, it also
hides from us its own reality as inertia, as autonomous materiality,
which is a barrier to the realization of our intentions, objectives, and
hopes.

This rescues the germ of truth in the notion of fetishism from the
tendentious interpretations advanced in the later Marxist tradition.
Despite asserting that fetishism or reification inheres in capitalist
commodity production, neither Marx nor any of his successors ever
showed that the commodity form itself prevents anyone understanding class relations in general, or domination, exploitation, and
injustice in particular. To be sure, some mystification about market
relations undoubtedly has afflicted some individuals and groups at
certain times and under specific circumstances. But from the late
nineteenth century onward, large sectors of the European working
classes have consistently opposed the unbridled operation of the
capitalist system, showing that the system of commodity production itself erected no general barrier to an understanding of its true
nature and limitations. Thus we have no good reason for believing
that the majority of people have been misled – in the sense of having made choices inconsistent with their own authentic desires – by
the fetishism described above.

Lukács's concept of reification also appears to have a different
significance in the light of Sartre's work. As indicated above, the
substance of reification is actually the process of rationalization
described by Weber: mechanization, routinization, quantitative
measure, and so forth. There is no doubt that this process of rationalization constitutes the new, fateful dimension of the world of

the practico-inert under the sway of industrialism. However, in compounding his notion of reification, Lukács simply appropriated the connotations of rationalization and attributed them quite arbitrarily to commodity production rather than to industrialization. When, following this operation, he substituted reification for fetishism, he simply magnified Marx's error.

Lukács opened his famous essay by referring to 'the reification produced by commodity relations.' But in his subsequent exposition he offered no convincing proof that commodity production generated reification. In fact, as we have seen, his argument turns (as Marx's does, but in different terms) on an implausible contrast between premodern and modern societies, with the suggestion that pre-capitalist societies enjoyed thoroughly non-reified social relations. To correct this misconception one simply has to reverse its terms. Commodity production is a specific instance – and industrialized commodity production a still more specific instance – of reification, that is, of the mediation of humans by things.

Finally, seen from this perspective, Marcuse projected onto modern technologies the quasi-autonomous character of the practico-inert. This is an error, for 'technological rationality' – Weber's formal rationality under a new name – is a necessary aspect of industrialization, no matter what type of social relations are involved. The characteristics of rationalization are increasingly the dominant characteristics of the sphere of the practico-inert in modern times.

The seductive proposal made by Lukács and Marcuse is that under socialism we could have the material blessings of industrialism and still shield social relations from the corrosive forces of rationalization and reification. This cannot be. Modern technology is part of an orientation for human action that alters radically the way in which the material exchanges between humanity and nature through labour are conducted.

This orientation is grounded in a wish to understand natural processes so thoroughly that we will be able to intervene in them at any point in order to turn the course of events to our advantage. Modern medicine provides a good specific illustration of this general orientation, which often is called our striving to 'conquer' nature. In modern society, many people consider sustained technological innovation to be visible proof of humanity's success in this endeavour. Yet there are a number of curious paradoxes hidden in this quest, some of which are explored in the next chapter.

6
DOMINION OVER NATURE:
IDOLS OF THE TRIBE

The idea that humanity can 'conquer' nature encapsulates some of the fondest hopes in modern industrial societies. Having received this notion from the religious heritage of Western civilization, modern societies proceeded to secularize it and to cherish it as an image of what separates them from the endemic frustrations of the past. Previous history is viewed as the rise and inevitable decline of successive civilizations, the new ones plundering the old and eventually being plundered in turn, an endless cycle of heroism and subsequent decay. The conquest of nature, however, promised to break that cycle and to lay permanent foundations for humanity's prosperity and progress. The idea took hold in the historical epoch often called the triumph of capitalism or 'business civilization'; but it has also been adopted more recently and with equal fervour in societies dedicated to the ideals of socialism and communism.

As an idea or ideology, the conquest of nature has become part of the system of values that express our most cherished collective aspirations. Its substantive foundations are the institutional arrangements that co-ordinate the following interrelated undertakings: systematic research in the natural sciences, rapid technological innovation, greatly enhanced extraction of resources and energy from the environment, and industrial manufacture. These undertakings are a great human accomplishment and, for many, constitute visible evidence of our success in conquering nature. More specifically, modern science is popularly regarded as the key element in this institutional complex: technology and industry use the fecund discoveries made in the laboratories to enhance human existence. This – our 'scientific culture' – binds the modern natural sciences to the popular aspirations for material well-being, relief from disease and illness, and continuous technological novelty.

We often also have second thoughts. Large numbers of people do live in improved circumstances, but most people on the globe still lack some of the basic necessities of life. A large proportion of that group is chronically undernourished, and some are simply starving. Many affluent nations have extensive environmental degradation, where material benefits are offset by ugliness, social tensions, and blighted natural surroundings. Finally, even some more affluent people feel relative deprivation: every stage of material progress brings new, unfulfilled wants that deny to many the contentment and well-being expected to accompany higher levels of consumption. Antagonisms stemming from the inequitable distribution of the benefits of industrial progress both within and among nations have not diminished as expected and indeed may be increasing.

These antagonisms form an endemic crisis in our own civilization and in the scientific culture that is such a vital aspect of it. So far most high-level advisers have responded by calling for more of the same: more scientific research, more technical innovations, more output. According to one contemporary prophet, an intensive program of this sort can provide material affluence for the ten or fifteen billion humans expected to inhabit the earth in the twenty-first century. If this program were to be attempted and did not succeed, the resulting disillusionment might undermine political institutions and the scientific culture that has become associated with this 'technological fix' approach.

The theoretical and experimental achievements of the modern natural sciences have been linked closely with our hopes for material affluence. This linkage is one of the most important ingredients in our scientific culture. If these hopes are dashed, how will this affect that scientific culture? We cannot assume that that culture will be entirely unaffected. Periodically we hear about the inflation of consumers' expectations in Western societies, which allegedly increases their economic difficulties. We may also experience the cumulative effect of a related collapse in expectations of the material well-being that was supposed to result from science and technology. If social stresses are severe, we may witness growing antipathy toward scientific method.

A protest that the blame is misplaced will not carry much weight in such circumstances. It will be too late then to urge that we should discriminate between the method of scientific inquiry and the shattered hopes for material well-being and social tranquillity with which (unfortunately) it had been associated. The scientific community, anxious for massive research funding, acquiesced in the promotion of unrealistic public expectations, such as the elimination of hunger throughout the world with the 'green revolution' or Richard Nixon's 'conquest of cancer' – it will be too late then to admit that this was unwise. Now is the time to begin making the necessary discriminations. Now is the time to begin detaching our scientific culture from the popular expectations associated with the conquest of nature and the technological fix.

We must divorce the actual endeavours of science from the misguided beliefs that humanity can and should seek 'dominion' over nature and that such dominion would assure social tranquillity. These misguided convictions blind us to the actual sources of turmoil – our social relations – and breed in us a reckless, indifferent attitude toward non-human nature, an attitude as harmful to ourselves as to the many other beings who share the earth with us.

In the following sections I shall explore two questions. What is meant by 'dominion over nature'? And what is meant by its opposite, respect for nature?

Science and Dominion

To understand the modern search for dominion over nature, we must first identify the role of science and then separate it from the other elements that make up this conception. We can start by examining the historical stages in the evolution of this idea from early modern times to the present.

We know that the idea of human dominion over nature has its deepest roots in the Judaeo-Christian religious tradition within Western civilization.[1] The prominent biblical sources, especially the book of Genesis, have kept this idea alive in the Western imagination for the last fifteen hundred years. Indeed, much of the most serious discussion of the relationship between humanity and nature stimulated during the past decade by the new interest in environmental issues has taken place in theological circles. Some commentators have emphasized the crucial ambiguities in the religious tradition, for example, the partially conflicting images of humans as rulers over nature and as stewards and guardians of nature. Many different interpretations of biblical imagery have been made in the history of Christian thought, and the contemporary contributions indicate just how vital this intellectual tradition remains in our culture.

For the problems of our scientific culture, however, there are three key questions. How and why was this religious imagery converted into secular terms? More specifically, how did modern science become linked with the secularized version of human dominion over nature? And what general social changes created the supportive medium in which the new version could take root and flourish?

The intellectual history of seventeenth-century Europe provides some good answers to these questions.[2] It was an exciting period, and not without danger for enterprising thinkers, who were left exposed to charges of heresy. Theology, alchemy, metaphysics, natural philosophy, and a rudimentary experimental science were in flux, producing intellectual innovations that were to help change the world – but which first had to be distilled from a vast outpouring of extravagant and sometimes bizarre theorizing. Dominating the controversies was the overriding necessity to reconcile novel concepts in natural philosophy with Christian theology.

Even a cursory glance at these sources shows us how many pitfalls and false turnings awaited the thinkers who were seeking a new synthesis of theology and natural philosophy. The inevitable mishaps brought great anguish to those like Mersenne who were devoted with equal passion to both religion and science. In view of the vast scope of these personal and social dilemmas, Francis Bacon's achievement in substantially resolving them is truly remarkable. Like many such achievements, his can appear in retrospect superficial and naïve; but Bacon hit on the one argument that would prove irresistible to his contemporaries: success in the scientific investigation of nature would be a 'sign' that mankind was once again proving itself morally worthy in the sight of God.

Bacon based this argument on a provocative reading of the Genesis story about the expulsion from Paradise. With its fall from divine grace, humanity lost two qualities: moral innocence and dominion (in the sense of unchallengeable power) over its earthly habitat. He then added an equally provocative reading of the appointed task of organized religion, namely, to 'repair' the loss of moral innocence – but not, strangely enough, the loss of dominion. This rather unorthodox (and perhaps heretical) theological position was stated as follows in *The New Organon*: 'For man by the fall fell at the same

time from his state of innocency and from his dominion over creation. Both of these losses however can even in this life be in some part
repaired; the former by religion and faith, the latter by arts and
sciences.'[3] This argument has an even more fascinating sequel: Bacon
asserts the moral innocence of the arts and sciences. This bold contention of a primordial bond between moral innocence and dominion over the earth effectively undermines the earlier, equal position
of institutionalized religion and institutionalized science. For now
regained dominion over the earth – which Bacon claims is within the
capacity of the human arts and sciences to produce – will indicate
that the loss of innocence is being repaired (which we may understand as the moral regeneration of the human species).

Ostensibly, Bacon had acknowledged the institutional priority of
religion within his program for raising dramatically the social importance of science in recovering dominion: 'Only let the human race
recover that right over nature which belongs to it by divine bequest,
and let power be given it; the exercise thereof will be governed by
sound reason and true religion.' But his argument (whether he was
aware of this or not is irrelevant) reversed the order of priority.
Indeed, with the implicit suggestion that a repaired dominion
through science would constitute visible evidence of a repaired innocence, it left open the way for the elimination of religion altogether
as a judge of the ethical worth of our endeavours – in other words,
for an exclusively secular understanding of human dominion over
nature.[4]

The way indicated by Bacon's work was eagerly followed by so
many others that by the nineteenth century the earlier religious
understanding had been eclipsed almost totally. The combined thrust
of science, technology, and industry was now seen as the sole vehicle
of dominion; this appeared so self-evident that from then onward
no argument on its behalf was thought necessary. However, this attitude incorporated some hidden assumptions with momentous implications even today not widely recognized.

In the religious version, human dominion over nature is grounded
in a larger moral order. Dominion was granted to humans only in
so far as they regulated their behaviour in accordance with a specified
pattern of relationships – and responsibilities – toward all entities
established by the Creator, and it was subsequently forfeited (for the
most part) when that original order was violated. Dominion was to
have regard to the whole network, not just to the isolated self-interest

of human agents: this is the message of the expulsion from the Garden. Dominion is lost when humans become estranged from God and from the original moral order.

Obviously our culture has little use for this traditional imagery today. But perhaps the account can be interpreted less literally. There is a proper place for our attempts to secure greater control over natural processes through science and technology. But if our search for dominion over nature ignores the integrity of the network of relationships among living entities, without any feeling that we belong to a community of beings who share the earth with us in our common habitat, this search for dominion may well become self-destructive. The sense of responsibility and community – 'respect for nature' – should help to shape and define the kind of dominion we seek.

What dominion over nature means without a complementary respect for nature is foreshadowed in the Baconian transformation discussed above. By identifying dominion with scientific and technological progress, Bacon loaded the metaphor of dominion with certain crucial assumptions that remained hidden from him and his eager followers down to the present day. These assumptions governed the way in which three related issues were formulated: the meaning of dominion itself, the alleged benefits of enlarged dominance for humanity, and the role of science (as the agency of dominion) in determining our conception of nature.

Dominion: Meaning, Benefits, Agency

With respect to the first issue, Bacon assumed that the secular variant of dominon would be strictly analogous to its religious model. An active agent could shape a passive material substratum according to the dictates of its utterly unhindered will. Humans could step into God's role as fully self-conscious beings able to organize the rest of nature, and completely control natural processes, so that nature could supply the material foundations for the fulfilment of all our desires. Knowledge of nature as the means of power over nature – the alchemists' heritage which Bacon disguised with the Christian images of fall from grace and redemption. Understanding natural processes would enable mankind to do whatever it willed to do: nature would become, in Bacon's words, the 'slave' of mankind.

There are at least two major and problematic assumptions built into this secular conversion of a theological model. One is what we might call the notion of an individed will. This is postulated in the very conception of a monotheistic deity. But dominion as imperious will, when transferred to and postulated of the human species, makes no sense. For the species itself is not united but rather is divided in countless ways (nationality, ethnicity, sex, age, social class, and so on), and every division conditions the perception of human aims and interests.

Even if the species were not so divided, it could never possess or exercise this kind of imperious dominion, since the latter presupposes a fully self-conscious will. Such a (hypothetical) will harbours no internal sources of tension or hidden autochthonous drives, no interplay between conscious and subconscious motives – precisely the opposite of human will. From actual human wills come conflicting and sometimes contradictory desires; for example, technological mastery over nature enhances life for some people and simultaneously degrades it for others. Imperious dominion over nature – over everything 'external' to mind or spirit – requires perfect transparency and unity of purpose in the will. This is neither possible nor desirable in human life. Thus humanity cannot 'step into' God's role as omnipotent ruler over nature.

The second assumption concerns a less speculative dimension; indeed, it has much practical significance. The concept of imperious dominion excludes in principle all unintended consequences of action, or what we have come to call 'negative externalities' – the unintended environmental and health hazards caused by our manipulations of natural processes. The proposition can be modified by conceiving dominion in a weaker sense, of course. Thus negative externalities would not be ruled out in principle, but we would assume that any harmful effects from them could be fully corrected by further manipulations.

Undoubtedly such corrections are possible in particular circumstances. But as our industrial technology becomes more complex and massive, employing exotic chemicals in great quantities, the environmental effects become equally complex and increasingly impinge upon large systems in the biosphere (the oceans and planetary weather patterns, for example). We do not yet know whether we can control and correct these systems and mitigate any adverse ecological reactions stemming from our alterations of them. What is clear is that the process is self-augmenting: the more extensive the initial impact is, the more wide-ranging are the necessary subsequent ad-justments – and so on. We simply do not know how this existing step-by-step approach will fare in the long run.

The second issue handed down to us in the Baconian legacy con-cerns the benefits of enlarged dominion. According to the accepted indicators of social progress, most people in industrialized nations enjoy a standard of living far superior to what obtained in preceding centuries. The continuing deprivations suffered by so many of the earth's inhabitants elsewhere are considered remediable by further application of the same industrial technology that brought prosperity to the fortunate minority – in fact, it is an added stimulus to our technological ingenuity. At regular intervals, estimates are offered of the date when we can except all the human race to attain current North American consumption levels and beyond.

The practical obstacles to fulfilment of this promise are enormous. How to deliver the tenfold increase in available resources and energy required to bring the world's population up to North American con-sumption levels? (And the world's population will rise at the same time.) The energy requirements alone would be staggering. Some experts also fear the climatic modifications that may result from the resulting environmental effects in the biosphere. One must at least acknowledge the uncertainties inherent in any effort to universalize the perceived material benefits of dominion.

The third issue concerns our vision of modern science as the agency of dominion. This vision is founded on the obvious connec-tion between an improved knowledge of physical transformations in nature and our increased capacity to use those transformations to achieve designated objectives. Science proceeds by penetrating deeper and deeper 'behind' the visible forms and the sensuous qualities of natural things to the common elements of which they are composed, ultimately reaching an ambiguous dimension where the borders between matter and energy – between substantial and in-substantial form – begin to disappear. It returns from this search with knowledge that permits us to mould the materials of nature into desired objects to an extent never before imagined. And we normally point to the practical results derived from such knowledge when we wish to explain dominion over nature.

There are two major problems here. The more immediate or down-to-earth problem involves the underlying popular expectations that buttress much of the public interest in and support for scientific research. In these expectations we can detect the residual force of the older impulses that once motivated the search for the philosopher's stone – the process that was thought to be the one key to all the powers and operations of nature. The eager anticipation of developments such as extracting unlimited quantities of energy from fusion reactors or eradicating all diseases and programming desired biological characteristics through genetic engineering, which are sometimes trumpeted by scientists as well as lay enthusiasts, reveals profound misunderstanding about what our science and technologies can do for us and, unfulfilled, may lead to growing hostility toward scientific inquiry and method.

The more abstract problem has to do with science's influential role in shaping our experience of nature. The progress of science has drawn our attention more and more forcefully to the fascinating (and useful) matter-energy transformations that occur beyond the reach of our unaided senses. It has helped to make our capacities for manipulating and recasting natural things of ever greater importance to us and has thereby become for many the measure by which to judge all science. But this conceptual imperialism is unhealthy for science as well as for us.

We apprehend the world differently in accordance with different modes of judgment. In the modern natural-science mode we abstract from sensuous qualities in order to locate the common structure of matter-energy transformations. Since this mode of apprehension facilitates our operational capacity to use those transformations in the service of our desires, many people have spoken of our achieving dominion over nature by these means. But the matter-energy fields represented by mathematical science cannot be regarded as a proxy for nature per se, or as nature's essential core.

We apprehend the world in sensuous immediacy as well as in mathematical constructions; neither method has better access to the 'reality' of nature. In music, dance, painting, and every art, humans have strived to preserve the duality of unbounded sensuousness and ordered pattern that the experience of nature presents to us in ordinary perception. The sensuous appearance of nature is just as much an expression of its significance for us as its atomic structure is. We could not live in a world without sensuous qualities. It makes no sense to speak of dominion over nature in this mode of apprehension, however.

Any careful consideration of these three issues – the meaning, benefits, and agency of dominion – must conclude by restricting the meaning of dominion over nature to a quite narrow compass. Non-human nature can never be rendered the slave of mankind; there are no unmixed blessings for mankind as a whole in the progress of scientific inquiry and technological applications; and the arts and sciences can never achieve dominion over nature as such. Once this is clearly understood and acknowledged, we can specify the positive attributes of a narrowly defined version.

Reconsiderations on Dominion

The superficial but prevalent conception of dominion over nature dissected above perpetuates a false image of ourselves, our science, and nature. First, the sum total of our aims and desires is not and cannot be sufficiently unambiguous as to allow us to direct our operational abilities so that their accomplishments fully satisfy our expectations. We must rather expect greater or lesser frustration at any level of technological sophistication and learn to restrain the immense demands we are now placing on the regenerative capacity of the planetary biosphere. Second, our natural sciences, which necessarily pursue their investigations within a limited range of concepts, can never grasp some ultimate or final truth of nature's being; they must recognize that other, radically different modes of apprehension are of equal importance in interpreting nature for us. Finally, nature must always be seen as being more than patterns of matter-energy transformations; its sensuous qualitites – the subtle plays of light, colour, sound, taste, and tactile sensation that produce an inexhaustible wealth of material for individual experience – constitute the living environment wherein we search for satisfaction and well-being.

If we accept these propositions in some form, can we then reformulate the notion of dominion over nature, or must we discard it altogether? I think it is appropriate to reformulate rather than to discard it. Even though the prevailing interpretation has helped to propagate certain false, even harmful images, it has also served some useful purposes.

In its rise to prominence the modern secular idea of human domination over nature overcame other philosophies of nature and other conceptions of the proper relationship between humanity and nature. Some of them had developed within Christian theology, and others were surviving remnants of archaic, pre-Christian beliefs. These earlier cosmologies are representative instances of a widespread pattern in human societies, namely, the striving to situate human existence within a larger order of meaningful associations embracing all natural entities.

As shared mythologies, they were bonds of social cohesion as well as interpretations of existence. These cosmologies also had regressive and sometimes oppressive features. Specific forms of social relationships arising out of specific historical circumstances – sex-role stereotypes, class and status divisions, kinship networks – were rationalized by situating them in the cosmological schemes; they too were said to be 'natural' and therefore eternal. The myths that explained the generation of plant and animal life explained in similar terms the established division of labour. In what we are wont to call 'primitive' societies, the social differentiation thus legitimized does not appear (in many cases at least) especially oppressive or exploitative; in other cases, and in all earlier 'civilizations,' the cosmologies sanctioned the barbarous treatment of oppressed groups by ruling elites.

We need not argue that the 'milder' forms of social differentiation, as opposed to the blatantly exploitative instances, were entirely or even largely detrimental for the individuals concerned. We cannot be as confident of the blessings of 'progress' as our forbears were, and thus we can assume that this pervasive practice of fixing social relations in the order of nature was an at least partially satisfactory response to deeply felt needs. Whatever our assessment of the net results, however, we can see everywhere around us the diminishing efficacy of this common mythological pattern. Its foundations have been undermined, perhaps irreparably, by the irresistable spread of industrial society, with its requirements for changes in the division of labour and indeed in social roles generally.

The accompanying newer mythology of dominion over nature undermines belief in those cosmologies as well. When nature is regarded as a purely external dimension which can be subjected to human will, nature cannot be thought to dictate either the pattern of social relations or the forms of relationships between humans and other entities. I have argued that the prevalent conception of dominion over nature is unacceptable; but I also believe that in helping to undermine the older cosmologies it has had a beneficial influence. To rationalize social relations by projecting them onto an image of nature, as older societies have done, or to rationalize an uncontrolled industrial technology as an instrument for the conquest of nature, as modern societies are wont to do, is equally unsatisfactory (for different reasons). Both are one-sided perspectives that impose on non-human nature excessively rigid structures derived from particular human interests.

In any event there is no turning back. If we wish to reformulate our inherited idea of dominion over nature, we should not do so by attempting to revive earlier models, all of which have their own defects. I have chosen to reformulate rather than to reject the concept of dominion over nature because I believe that certain aspects of it should be preserved. What we should preserve is the resistance embodied in the concept against projecting forms of social relations onto the natural order, a process that distorts our perceptions of both society and nature. By examining the concept of respect for nature, we may be able to discover how to go about this without succumbing to the equally grave distortions transmitted to us in the Baconian legacy.

Harmony with Nature?

Those who have found fault with the concept of dominion over nature have proposed various substitutes. The most popular seems to be the suggestion that we should live in a state of harmony with nature. This notion presents certain difficulties of its own, however. Since any significant measure of human activity must have some environmental impact, it is unclear at what point – and from whose point of view – a harmonious accord with our surroundings has been either attained or breached. In practical terms this notion is usually associated with pre-industrial pastoral life, or at least a form of life 'simpler' (in terms of demands for industrial goods) than what exists today. Some people may believe that so-called primitive peoples who viewed animals as possessing spirits lived in greater harmony with nature than we now do; maybe so, but the natural ecosystems that sustained their ways of life might have been still more harmonious in the absence of any human settlements whatsoever.

Obviously harmony, like dominion, is a metaphorical expression. It is unwise to rely too heavily on either of them to derive practical guidelines for our behaviour. Harmony with nature – or respect for nature, the alternative expression used in this chapter – can be a metaphorical counterweight to dominion over nature, as a label to identify our reformulation of the latter. Before turning to that task, however, I would like to indicate some of the ways it should not be used.

As a result of the increasing sensitivity to environmental problems during the past decade, we have been urged to have greater respect for nature in a variety of senses. These conceptions have been drawn primarily from three historical sources: philosophies of 'resignation,' with roots in Christian theology; the natural philosophies that arose in the older civilizations of Japan, China, and India; and the 'Romantic' reaction to the industrial revolution. In addition to the popular commentaries that trivialize these sources, more serious thinkers who draw on them have raised ethical and metaphysical issues of continuing importance. Since I am concerned here only with what I take to be the popular understanding of these issues in our culture, not with the sophisticated philosophical and religious literature, I will comment only on how respect for nature is usually conceived at this level.

'Nature knows best': this timeworn phrase is about as good a summary of conventional wisdom as any. In this form respect for nature means either not interfering at all with so-called natural processes such as diseases, or only using so-called natural or organic substances, as opposed to industrially created chemicals. There are two basic errors in this attitude. First, human social organization represents an inescapable interference with the order of nature. Unlike other animals who also have forms of social organization, human cultures transmit through successive generations a far more elaborate collection of learned behaviour patterns, which condition responses to fluctuations in environmental conditions. Thus even in primitive societies changes in human populations are in no way comparable to predator-prey cycles, for instance, among other animals. To put the point crudely: we obey not nature but rather our conception of nature.

Second, the naïve preference for natural instead of industrially produced substances – common among 'health-food' devotees – is based on an inadequate knowledge of chemistry. Traditional pre-industrial techniques, including the uses of plant materials, are based on chemical and biological reactions learned through trial-and-error experiments rather than laboratory analyses; some are indeed both appropriate and beneficial, some have neutral health consequences, and some we know to be downright harmful. Our industrial techniques likewise produce results ranging from beneficial to harmful. One cannot distinguish the two different sets of effects using the categories of natural v. unnatural or artificial. Finer discriminations are necessary.

One can reasonably prefer vegetable over aniline dyes, for example, for at least two different reasons: they yield more pleasing colours (according to some tastes), and they are probably more benign, in terms of their unintended environmental effects, as we produce and consume them. One can also reasonably prefer the taste of the humble backyard tomato over that of its recent rival, the fruit of genetic engineering designed to produce a shape and skin thickness suitable for mechanical pickers. But one can also appreciate the quite sensible improvements in sanitation, comfort, and convenience wrought by industrial technology that genuinely contribute to our well-being.

Respect for Nature

Respect for nature should not be based on a blanket rejection of science-based technology and a fallacious belief that following the natural course of events is the best guideline for our behaviour. Equally as fallacious, I have suggested, is the view that we can expect our science and technology eventually to achieve such mastery over natural processes that we shall be able to pursue whatever whim happens to overtake us. But is there a middle ground? I believe so. Our scientific culture can entertain a rational conception of respect for nature, and this in turn can help the larger culture based on our industrial technology to modify its course in practical affairs.

Modern science allows us better understanding of how natural processes occur than other natural philosophies do. While we should not regard this as the only valid interpretation of what nature signifies to us, it will be and should be one significant mode of our relationship with non-human nature from now on. We understand much better than in the past the immense biological and chemical complexity of our physical environment and the species that inhabit it. We can make good use of this knowledge; but we need not assume that we can or should 'control' those complex interactions fully. Rather we could conclude, on the basis of our scientific knowledge, that there are far too many risks involved in attempting to manipulate larger and larger sets of ecological interactions for the sake of ephemeral short-run benefits.

In a very real sense our industrial technology's chemical wizardry is out of control. It tempts us with innumerable trivial novelties; it degrades the quality of our preferences, for example, by presenting bizarre laboratory concoctions to us and calling them foods; it is shockingly careless with toxic substances like the dioxin that showered the Italian town of Seveso; and it has not the slightest idea what the long-range synergistic effects of all these apparently clever techniques may be. As willing consumers of so much junk we co-operate fully and freely with this irresponsible enterprise, for most people are quite content to remain utterly unaware of the risks we run. So long as we prefer to accept without proper scrutiny whatever appears on the store shelves, the structure of oligopolistic market competition will require all producers to take part in provisioning the chemical feast for us.

Our social institutions have severely limited capacities for assimilating complex information sources in public decision-making processes. These limitations govern the practical impact of scientific knowledge on social, economic, and political choices. As we raise the levels at which we attempt to manipulate ecological interactions, we increase enormously the number of variables that must be controlled as well as the magnitude of the possible negative externalities that may appear. We may or may not have adequate theoretical models for identifying the key variables at any time; but even it we do, there is always the danger of overloading the practical capacity of our social institutions to carry out any necessary remedial measures.

For example, some scientists have argued that current human activities are causing the biotic diversity of the planet (the total number of different plant and animal species) to shrink at a progressively faster rate and that some harmful consequences might result. This is a highly speculative matter, and we cannot be sure whether this is the case, or, if it is, whether it will prove harmful. Here is an instance where our scientific understanding can advise us (as it has) to adopt the prudent course of seeking to decrease the environmental impact of our activities in order to minimize the possibility of long-range deleterious effects that we may not be able to contain or mitigate. We might choose to call this an instance of respecting the 'integrity' or autonomy of nature.

As it achieves a more comprehensive grasp of nature's complexity, scientific knowledge may help us to realize the practical impossibility of manipulating large-scale ecological interactions. If it does, and if we accept the restraint, this would be an example of what I mean by a rational conception of respect for nature. It does not deny that we possess the 'power' – the scientific and technological capacity – to undertake those operations; rather it would mean that, with full knowledge that we do have the necessary instruments, we had recognized the limitations of our own nature as well as those of our social institutions and had chosen not to use those instruments for certain purposes.

Our cherished position as the earth's dominant species hardly would suffer as a result. We would still cover the planet with our settlements and continue to modify or destroy the habitats of other species along with some of the species themselves. Respect for nature through renunciation of large-scale environmental manipulations would start as the most prudent course for the long-term preservation of our own well-being. It would also have appreciable spin-off benefits for other living entities by reducing both the direct and indirect pressures we exert on them. This would be at first only an unintended consequence of a more enlightened pursuit of self-interest for ourselves; but in time we might find that seeing ourselves as members of a community of living entities, rather than as unchallengeable masters of a conquered domain, yields a finer sense of contentment and well-being than we have been able to find on our present heading.

There is an old idea of humanity as steward of nature in the Christian tradition. A secular version of this idea may be an appropriate adjunct to a rational conception of respect for nature. We have already modified most of the habitats on this planet, and we are well on our way toward completing the process; we are in a position to control or eliminate many (or perhaps any) other species through predation, modification or habitats, or genetic manipulation. In a very real sense, therefore, we are 'responsible' for the fate of all living things.

For some people it would be sufficient to reserve a few specimens of those that appeal to us in zoos and to let the rest take their chances. This is a rather limited notion of stewardship. A more generous interpretation would be to preserve as much as possible of the remaining habitats, with suitable compensation to those nations and groups whose economic interests are injured as a consequence.

Respect for nature as the excercise of voluntary restraint on our operational capacity to manipulate the environment has another aspect: respect for the full range of possible human experience in our relation to nature. The ever greater predominance of seeking operational control over nature in our culture restricts our experience of non-human nature to the dimension of matter-energy transformations expressed as 'laws' governing natural processes. But the numbers and material demands of the species grow at an equal or faster rate, always renewing the violent struggles over the spoils of dominion. No amount of operational control can resolve this dilemma; any hope of doing so resides only in a reordering of social relations. The industrialized nations should have accumulated enough evidence by now to realize that their existing political economy generates fresh material demands with each new level of production; these escalating demands intensify the search for further advances in operational techniques. Other dimensions of possible experience are repressed under the weight of this self-perpetuating exercise. To understand the necessity for restraining our operational capacities is to open the way toward a fuller and more balanced experience of nature.

Respect for nature really means respect for our own nature, for the full range of experience of which it is capable – and for its limitations as well. As of now we simply do not know whether it is possible (even if it were desirable) for us to manage adequately, through our social institutions, the full effects of the large-scale global ecological impacts, such as ozone depletion or the 'greenhouse effect,' that appear to be occurring as a result of using industrial technologies. And yet, however daunting this prospect seems to be, it is only our firm resolve, exercised through public policies ratified by popular authority, to bring the social effects of technologies into line with the values we respect that can preserve our freedom to make choices about our future. Part II explores ways in which we can protect this freedom against the pressures of the technological imperative.

PART TWO
MAKING CHOICES

7
TECHNOLOGY AND
THE ENVIRONMENT

I n his *Report of the Mackenzie Valley Pipeline Inquiry* (1977), Mr Justice Thomas Berger recommended that no energy corridor be permitted in the coastal region of northern Yukon. He proposed creation of a national park in that area – an idea accepted some time later by the federal government – that would 'afford absolute protection to wilderness and the environment by excluding all industrial activity within it.' The park will protect an area vital to maintenance of the Porcupine caribou herd, snow geese and other birds, fish, and many other wildlife species.

On the day the Berger report was released, television networks sought responses from Canadians on its principal recommendations. Quite understandably, since this was still a time of fears about energy shortages, many people erroneously interpreted the proposal as a denial of arctic natural gas to southern Canada. One Toronto suburban couple, asked whether they would if necessary forgo natural gas for their home for the sake of Yukon caribou, replied with barely concealed outrage: 'It's them or us.'

Echoing this mixture of indignation and bewilderment are some of the most fascinating paradoxes of contemporary society. After centuries of industrial development and 'conquest of nature,' after elimination of most of the wildlife and their habitats on the North American continent, we find that we cannot afford to become sentimental about some of the remaining caribou and geese who unwisely choose to breed near substantial fossil-fuel deposits. Were we not in such dire need of these substances we would, of course, be happy to consign that unpleasant territory to them and the few peculiar humans who apparently like living there. The needs of the industrial machine, like those needs it services, know no natural bounds.

The chief paradox is the pervasive insecurity of a society whose economy's material output is so abundant, as measured by most standards derived from past human history. The larger this output becomes, the more carefully it must be watched, and governments today have little time for anything except nursing the gross national product. Our insecurity stems mainly from the curious impermanence of what we want and how we produce it. Very little in our system is self-renewing save the wants that drive it on, and thus we must search in ever more remote places with escalating costs and more esoteric technologies for materials and energy to feed it.

The prevailing rules in our regulated market economy encourage rapid turnover of wants and products; industrial concentration and complex technologies make available for such purposes hitherto inaccessible deposits of the earth's resources. Prodigious waste of those resources seems to be a necessary function of this accelerating turnover, this impermanence of wants and products. (Barry Commoner estimates that we waste 85 per cent of the capacity to do useful work inherent in the energy we use.[1]) Conservation, recycling, and reuse are cumbersome tasks and delay the appearance of 'new' things. This profligacy has its price: will we have enough for the next round? Collective insecurity mounts in proportion to the growing heaps of half-used artifacts and momentary impulses flung into the surrounding waste-management sites.

Another paradox arises immediately out of the relation between technology and environment. Most environmental effects in the economically developed world stem directly from the operational capacities of our science and technologies, for example, new chemical compounds being dispersed in air and water or large-scale construction projects. For the most part we wish to deal with environmental issues only when we are forced to do so – that is, when some particular, adverse effect of our scientific and technological capacity makes itself felt. The rest of the time we are content pretty much to take the benefits (preferably at not too dear a price) and to put out of mind the vast range of transformations in chemistry, physics, and biology that are occurring around us. Briefly put, we would like the environment not to bother us.

What Is Environmental Impact?

More specifically, what are here referred to as 'environmental issues' are generally problems arising from (1) the effects of different technologies (especially industrial technologies) on the regenerative capacity of natural ecosystems and on human health, and (2) the effects – on both human societies and non-human species – of modifying habitats for settlements or other uses. The political aspects of environmental issues conern what we choose to do (or not do) about those issues – the degree of importance we attach to them, how well we understand the effects, and what effect our attending to them has on our institutions and social relations.

In one sense everything we do has an environmental impact: each of us at every moment is involved in complex interactions involving the organic and inorganic chemistry of nature. Most of these interactions do not, except trivially, give rise to environmental issues. Focusing of interest and awareness makes something an issue.[2] Thus issues normally arise with respect to well-developed social problems. Statements of issues can misrepresent a problem entirely, and pseudo-issues invent both the problem and its putative solution simultaneously.

When a set of issues first comes to wide public attention – as environmental issues did in the late 1960s – it can have a dual significance. There are expectations for solutions to immediate practical problems and also for changes in long-standing patterns of social development. Thus in the 1970s and 1980s we have seen highly practical demands (such as for better air- and water-quality standards) and more frequent discussions of long-range perspectives in human ecology, ethology, sociobiology, and so forth.

The reasons why heightened sensitivity to particular issues occurs at a certain point are difficult to determine. Familiar events come to be seen as a pattern, and we then *construct* a new way of seeing the interrelationships among things. For example, sex-role stereotyping in the workplace can be taken for granted until these conditions are understood as part of a socialization pattern that permeates an entire culture. Simply reversing the visual imagery connected with a familiar pattern, as was done for sexual stereotyping in Norman Lear's short-lived soap opera series *All That Glitters*, can enable us to see suddenly and more clearly not just a particular issue but also many other features in our social relationships as well.

For many people a heightened sensitivity to environmental issues also has meant a new way of seeing connections among different concerns. Air and water pollution, waste of resources, occupational health hazards, and the extinction of wildlife species began to be seen as elements of a pattern of social action built on both institutional arrangements and deeply rooted collective attitudes. Familiar doctrines and events were cast in a new light and fell into place in the new pattern. A good example is Lynn White's famous 1966 lecture, 'The Historical Roots of Our Ecological Crisis,' which placed contemporary environmental concerns in the context of Western religion. His essay created a minor sensation and has been reprinted in almost every collection on environmental issues published since.

The new way of seeing things can, however, become the exclusive way: everything now appears an illustration of this one pattern. It runs the risk of falling victim to the laws of fashion and so of being superseded by another intellectual innovation. Initial enthusiasm is perhaps inevitable but must be tempered gradually if the new perspective is to avoid this fate. If it claims to illuminate a hitherto obscure pattern of thought and action, it must also be modest enough to recognize the legitimate claims of other ways of seeing the world.

Neither our market economy nor our methods of public decision-making, for example, were designed with environmental concerns in mind. Our political economy responds to those concerns on the basis of well-established private interests, distribution of power, lines of authority, and ideologies. Its 'instinctive' response to environmental concerns is to define problems according to the capacity of existing institutions to deal with them – in this case, by extending existing regulatory and price mechanisms to deal more adequately with pollution.

Types of Environmental Problems

In general there are two kinds of environmental problems, quantitative and qualitative. In the first group I place all those that are approached through investigations in the natural sciences and to which we seek to attach some quantitative measure. For example, we try to identify the toxic substances that circulate in the environment as a result of our producing and consuming activity, to establish permissible levels of concentration for them, to find ways of regulating those levels, and to take remedial action where necessary.

Broader ecological studies investigate the synergistic effects of combined biochemical effects and biological interactions among large numbers of species and inorganic materials, in small and large ecosystems, so that we can regulate and mitigate effects both for humans and for other species. In the remainder of this chapter I shall deal primarily with the qualitative and social dimensions of environmental issues.

The qualitative problems are those arising out of our changing perceptions of what is called the quality of life. Our judgments in this domain also can be based in part on scientific inquiry and quantitative data – for example, in identifying medical problems associated with high noise levels or in recording the flora and fauna that inhabit a marsh. But below the threshold of obvious psychological disturbance, how important to us is a reasonably quiet home environment, where it is still possible to identify the bird's call above the traffic din? Just how important to us is the local marsh when the developer's bulldozers are poised on its periphery? How important is the distant habitat of an endangered species when discoveries of mineral wealth are made there? Does it really matter to us whether or not the blue whale or a butterfly species becomes extinct?

Environmental alterations change our conception of the quality of life in exceedingly subtle ways. Once a wildlife species becomes extinct or the local marsh is filled in and paved over, succeeding human generations cannot experience their presence (except in films and books) and therefore do not miss them. In other words, the perceived quality of life for most people in these generations is not diminished as a result of past environmental alterations. Such matters are intangible and are difficult to represent; they are all too easily dismissed – when they appear to conflict with tangible benefits such as cheaper energy or new housing – as the snobbish concerns of privileged elites.

Manifest and Latent Dimensions

The difficulties in conceptualizing quality-of-life issues, particularly the distribution of benefits and costs associated with them, indicate that the political side of environmental concerns has two principal aspects as well. These I call the 'manifest' and the 'latent' politics of environmental issues. On the manifest level, environmental matters enter the social and political arena as one among many sets of private and public interests, jostling for attention with other determinants of well-being: love, wealth, income, status, power, authority, respect. These interests make up an intricate web of associations for individuals, and normally one of them is separated out only when something appears to upset the existing balance of factors that constitutes the individual or social definition of well-being.

If any northern Canadian pipeline had been rejected on account of so-called environmental considerations, and if relative prices for natural gas supplies subsequently had risen, would the price change have significantly affected everyone, or only poorer groups? If mitigating environmental effects increases costs of constructing pipelines, will the increased costs of fuel affect everyone equally, or principally lower-income groups?[3] Where there are wide diversities in shares of income and wealth, as there are in Canadian society, public policies always have a differential effect on individual lives unless they are accompanied by offsetting measures such as subsidies. This differential effect determines the responses to all social issues, including environmental concerns.

With respect to this manifest layer of politics, environmental concerns will be – and must be – perceived as only one of the factors affecting one's well-being. Responses to those concerns will be routed along the various avenues – determined by one's position in the hierarchy of economic and political power – by which individuals seek to maintain and enhance their perceived well-being. With new, very general issues (like environmental problems), there is a strong tendency to define the issue as narrowly as possible. We find security in defining environmental problems quantitatively, as in permissible levels in parts per million or billion or trillion of substances, such as lead in ambient air and PCBs (polychlorinated biphenyl compounds) in fish. There now exists a general consensus on the need for regulatory standards for obviously toxic substances and on public responsibility for administering them – at least until the results hurt economic interests, at which point we sometimes shop around for the best bargain (the least disturbing statistical evidence) in the scientific data.

The latent politics of environmental issues involves, as well as qualitative judgments, the incalculable risks we run in the massive environmental transformations occurring everywhere as a result of industrialization and economic modernization. We like to think that we are increasingly able to control social and environmental change through democratic public policies shaped by scientific knowledge. But perhaps the very nature of a political economy founded on a complex industrial technology may prevent effective control of public policy by informed citizens.

Our political economy has introduced, as a feature of everyday life, rapid change in our experiences and expectations as well as in our social and natural environments. The prevailing ethos in our social surroundings, where such changes make themselves felt, helps condition individual behaviour and affects individuals' choices and preferences. Much of today's popular culture is made up of quick turnovers in preferences – ever-changing fashions, consumption styles, and new products. In this setting the sense of well-being is influenced most strongly by whatever political program promises to ensure uninterrupted economic prosperity. And, while many people if asked will testify to their concern for environmental protection, there is somewhat weaker support for decisive action and the expenditure of public funds to provide it.

Diminished sensitivity to environmental problems is a serious matter for a modern industrial economy that pumps out an endless stream of market-place novelties from its chemical wizardry. There is simply no time to do adequate environmental impact studies of the many thousands of new compounds (even if it were possible): we cannot wait for the new goods. Chlorofluorocarbon (CFC) propellants from aerosol sprays are already in the atmosphere, and polychlorinated biphenyl (PCB) compounds are in the water; we can only hope that adverse effects will be manageable. The old adage 'Out of sight, out of mind' is the perfect motto for those who believe that 'the environment' should not pester us with its problems. At times some persons in high positions toss off ideas – such as the antarctic ice mass as an ideal dump site for radioactive wastes from nuclear plants – hoping that no one will notice and thus that a quick solution to a nasty little problem may be found.

There is no known way of recovering substances such as PCBs once they are dispersed in our air, water, and soil, and apparently we shall have to monitor their effects indefinitely. The 300,000 tons of arsenic waste (a gold-processing byproduct) now stored in abandoned gold-mine shafts near Yellowknife may leach into surrounding water bodies should permafrost thawing occur: 'The Yellowknife reports said that the waste does not present an immediate problem as long as it is watched carefully. However, there were fears that when the mine eventually closes, it will flood. Flood waters would melt the permafrost and the arsenic might seep out into Great Slave Lake, a huge body of water connected with major northern river systems. The Environment Department is said to have recommended that the temperature of the permafrost be checked constantly and that the storage shafts be pumped forever so no flooding occurs. A Northern Affairs official in Yellowknife was quoted as saying that checks were to have been made from time to time but the federal Treasury Board never had approved a budget for the project.'[4] What kinds of guarantees can be given that the shafts will be pumped 'forever'? And how many other, similar situations are there that should be 'watched carefully'?

How could we have known, when as sovereign consumers we expressed our preference for pressurized cans over manual-pump spray containers, that the gases that saved us the exertions of our fingers would rise through the atmosphere to react with ozone? (What is ozone anyway?) How could we have known, when inserting carbon paper into our typewriters or switching on fluorescent lights, that later, decomposing in our garbage, they would allow PCBs (whatever they might be) to seep into our rivers and lakes and to become more highly concentrated along the food chain, until the reproductive rate of herring gulls and double-breasted cormorants dropped sharply and until governments advised 'all women capable of pregnancy' (at least those who read government bulletins) not to eat any fish brought home from their husbands' outings on Lake Ontario?

With these randomly chosen examples in mind, try to imagine the kind of bureaucratic apparatus that might be required adequately to enforce environmental standards for thousands of potentially harmful chemicals: studying their intended and unintended biological actions, estimating the risks of adverse effects, monitoring their movement through ecosystems and species, regulating their uses in industrial plants, informing the public about hazards, compensating individuals and businesses for losses, and funding medical remedies for exotic complaints.

The latent politics of environmental issues is defined most sharply by the case of environmental standards. By 1975 the US Food and Drug Administration had set a limit of five parts per million for PCB concentrations in fish for human consumption (at that time Canada had no regulations on the matter).[5] The International Joint Commission, a US-Canadian advisory agency on water bodies, proposed a limit of one part per trillion – in effect, a zero limit. For PCBs and many other known or suspected hazards, even when we have at our disposal a raft of scientific studies, there remains an irreducible portion or uncertainty about what standard is necessary for protecting human health and environmental quality.

But the Great Lakes have a considerable commercial and sports-fishing industry that was already suffering losses because of regulations on other chemical contaminants. A US official told a reporter that technical experts were asked for 'a number that would not badly impact economic interests' during discussions on more stringent standards for PCBs. This theme recurs constantly in published reports about changes in environmental standards – for asbestos, lead, radioactive materials, and many others. The political process mediates temporary trade-offs among a wide range of considerations, including the costs of scientific research and data monitoring, unemployment, capital investment, public awareness, and rates of occupational disease. The 'number' selected for an environmental standard only appears to be derived directly from the pure disinterested inquiries of the laboratory; in fact, it usually represents a rough compromise among vested interests, balancing science, politics, and economy on the knife-edge of potential catastrophe.[6]

How Environmental Issues Arose

In the manifest politics of environmental issues, environmental hazards are one among many factors in the conflicting play of social interests. Accepting this was bitter fare for those who imagined in the first flush of excitement over the discovery of 'spaceship earth' that the magic term 'ecology' would still the endemic clamour over how to parcel out the planet's booty. It is instructive to review how various currents converged to heighten sensitivity to environmental concerns, why established institutional processes inevitably domesticated this new sensitivity, and finally what the changed alignment of interests represented.

Many divergent sources came together in the 1960s to turn environmental problems into a major social issue. I have isolated five of these sources below, but there were also others. After describing each briefly, I shall discuss various institutional responses to the issue of the environment.

First, 'the environment' was simply a new label for some very old problems in industrial society. The horrible effects of unhealthy working conditions in mines and factories are the most persistent; despite significant improvements over the years, largely forced onto the statute books by labour struggles, this remains one of the worst blights on our social record. Even the very diagnosis of hazards still entails a battle against bureaucratic resistance, including the pitiful spectacle of attempts by workers' widows to marshal medical evidence of occupationally caused deaths before sceptical compensation boards. Medical science has neglected occupational disease, so that reliable, relevant statistics rarely exist. Yet even if they were available, such quantitative measures could convey not even the slightest impression of the individual suffering represented in them. Those who doubt this should consult books such as Elliott Leyton's *Dying Hard*, which records the slow, agonizing deaths, in their families' presence, of Newfoundland men poisoned in the fluorspar mines. 'Simple' things like noise, dust, and heat take their toll, along with asbestos, vinyl chloride, and lead, as the hidden human cost of profit and industrial wealth.

Second, the new label for these old problems highlighted particular instances as part of a pattern of abuse inflicted on people – the population as a whole, or in certain occupational settings – and other living entities. Air pollution and water pollution are the most widely recognized cases. The larger picture revealed the environmental context of diseases such as cancer and the interconnections among different health problems related to general factors such as stress in our social environment.

Third, heightened sensitivity permitted us to detect or better appreciate some hitherto unknown or obscure matters. We learned much more about the increasing concentration of toxic chemicals through the various stages in the food chain (levels of chlorinated compounds are 40,000 times higher in fish than in the waters they inhabit, and the concentrations increase in the birds and polar bears that in turn feed on them). Research in atmospheric chemistry led to controversies over aerosol sprays, supersonic aircraft, and the shrinking of the Amazon forest. Dedicated followers of these and similar episodes discovered many things formerly little known, such as the vast quantities of antibiotics routinely administered to animals raised for human consumption, eventually – it seems likely – increasing resistance to drug treatment of disease organisms. And so on.

After digesting a certain amount of such information one reaches a threshold limit, and a mildly catatonic state may ensue. So the knowledge that one's lowly beer has been treated with twenty-five chemical additives (including one to inhibit foaming when it is un-capped and another to produce foaming when it is poured into the glass) no longer registers, and one orders another, which seems to help matters considerably.

Fourth, some existing problems were exacerbated by greater at-tention. The more indiscriminate attacks launched by environmental groups on pollution or on energy-generation facilities have been met with accusations that such groups were indifferent to the plight of the poor and the unemployed, who would be most severely affected by higher prices and construction delays. The ritual burial of a brand-new automobile in the United States was furiously denounced, and independent California loggers expressed in no uncertain terms their displeasure over filling out environmental impact assessment forms for cutting trees. The 1970 Stockholm Conference erupted in accusa-tions that environmental protection was only the latest stratagem in the industrialized world's plot to keep developing nations as raw-material suppliers. The exporting of pollution, for example the dumping of toxic wastes from European nations in African countries, has begun to cause some serious confrontations.

Finally, many individuals reordered their priorities concerning social change. After the first wave of initial enthusiasm passed, many people remained dedicated to long-range efforts to investigate en-vironmental problems and to help our institutions deal with them effectively. Campaigners on behalf of whales and seals can receive wide publicity, leading to accusations of theatrical posturing. But thousands also work productively and more quietly for governments, public interest groups, corporations, and universities. Popular and academic literature, television, film, and other media have com-municated the results with increasing effectiveness, and at the very least we now seem to have public resolve to include environmental considerations in all important policy choices. Opinion polls show that the Canadian public consistently rates environmental protec-tion as one of its highest concerns.

These dimensions of an emerging issue, I believe, reveal more than a passing fad. I do not think that we shall ever again (except perhaps under extreme social stress) ignore environmental effects in deciding major policy questions – a significant change in our social con-sciousness. I am not claiming that the major features of our political economy and social relations have been altered thereby. Our political economy would of course seek to contain environmental concerns within its own limits. These limits are the capacity of existing institutions to manage problems so as not to threaten unduly the general alignment of established social interests, such as the distribution of wealth and power.

Setting aside speculation about the significance of environmental concerns in the future, we can ask what the institutional responses to this issue tell us about those institutions themselves.

Institutional Responses

Specialists in comparative politics study institutional responses as an index of variations in political systems.[7] Comparing institutional adjustments to pollution-abatement programs in the United States, the Soviet Union, and Japan, for example, can show us which interest groups or professions in each country can influence policy decisions. In addition we can see how bureaucratic agencies adjust both to new information and to pressures from citizens' initiatives.

For example, since the mid-1970s there has been considerable public controversy over nuclear energy development in many Western nations. (East Germany simply announced that this was a non-issue and that nuclear power would assist the continued march of socialism.) In Great Britain and Canada, citizens' groups participated extensively in official inquiries, and the contributions of public interest organizations and concerned individuals are being taken into account. However, no such opportunities traditionally have been presented in France or West Germany; violent public demonstrations there are caused at least in part by governments' failure to provide other avenues for expression of dissent against established policies.

In economic affairs the path of least resistance is to adjust market forces to deal with more stringent pollution standards and related requirements. The additional expense of better anti-pollution equipment is therefore included in the costs of production, sometimes resulting in higher prices for consumers. But there are other, less obvious changes as well. Adjustments to more elaborate environmental impact regulations and to capital investment expenditures for pollution-abatement equipment may be easier for large corporations than for small or medium-sized firms. Thus one unintended consequence of allowing market forces to govern the economic effects of improved environmental standards may be to augment the already considerable thrust toward greater concentration of economic power.

At the same time, the world-wide scope of operations by multinational corporations limits the ability of national governments to enforce stricter environmental regulations. When Canadian provinces lowered permissible levels of concentration in plants processing asbestos, corporations transferred the 'dirtier' operations to those Third World countries whose compliant authorities were willing to trade off health hazards and economic benefits in a way no longer acceptable in Canada.

Threats to local employment and capital investment have been cited almost always in response to environmental concerns about large-scale manufacturing, mining, or energy-production facilities. Labour union leaders and members have usually stood shoulder-to-shoulder with corporation executives in dismissing or in seeking to minimize such concerns. Sometimes unions have disagreed among themselves over these matters. In Britain the leader of the Yorkshire coal miners, appearing at a public inquiry into the safety of fast-breeder nuclear reactors, argued that these reactors present an extreme environmental hazard; Britain could avoid developing them, he suggested, and instead rely on increased coal supplies for generating electricity until solar energy could help fulfil energy needs in the coming century. He was vigorously opposed by the union representing nuclear station employees, which denied that these generating plants were environmentally hazardous – and emphasized the occupational disease and accident records of coal miners.

Finally, how have governments reacted to the new social issue? Here one must admire the elegant simplicity of the initial response: a ministry (department) of the environment. Like good dance troupes, experienced governments can come up with a new act on very short notice. When they perceive the situation as only a matter of riding out a storm, this bureaucratic choreography can be quite amusing. One Italian government created and then dismantled a department of the environment within a mere eight months. In Canada the federal department was once paired with Fisheries – perhaps a less inspired union than the provincial ministries that join 'culture' with sport or recreation. When governments change in Canada – for example, after the 1984 federal election – environment departments curiously seem to bear the brunt of hastily conceived demands for changes in organizational structures, programs, and priorities. In Britain, the secretary of state for the environment is responsible for ancient monuments and historic buildings, driver-licence examinations, town planning, and parks, as well as for air and water quality and toxic chemicals.

The rather hasty manner in which older regulatory bodies, such as air-quality and water resources boards, were patched together under a present-day rubric certainly impaired the effectiveness of such new bureaucratic conglomerates. Housing various branches in the same office tower may create the illusion of co-ordination, but carrying out a co-ordinated approach in practice is another matter entirely. The obstacles are compounded by noble statutes, such as Ontario's 1975 Environmental Assessment Act, which potentially subjects every impingement on the environment (that is, every human action) to the watchful eye of government; common sense, and the substantial interests of other ministries, confine its application to a rather more narrow range of problems. Yet it is certainly useful, from a public-relations standpoint, for governments to claim that a designated line of responsibility for environmental matters of every conceivable kind has been established.

I have offered only a few illustrations of institutional responses to environmental issues in four areas (political systems, business, labour organizations, and government administration). Two different approaches have been indicated. We can use the perspective of environmental concerns to shed light on the internal dynamics of these institutions, whatever their concerns. With regard to environmental specifics – permitted levels of toxic substances in air and water, for example – we can assess the responses of existing institutions to the problems as we now understand them.

Institutions respond to issues (or ignore them) by balancing two kinds of pressures: those emanating from what we might call their 'deep structure,' which represents the historical sediment of the most influential social class and ideological forces, and current expressions of perceived self-interest by individuals and groups that seek to influence policies. The degree of flexibility in institutions, that is, the extent to which they can effectively confront new issues, varies considerably from one society to another.

Responses to environmental issues in North America reveal both the extent and the limits of institutions' adaptability. Shortly after the potential danger of chlorofluorocarbon propellants was reported, manufacturers offered manual-pump spray containers once again, and in advertising them they pointed out how much more economical they were for consumers! The balancing of pressures with respect to mercury pollution in northern Ontario rivers has been far less imaginative, to say the least. Providing a dole of frozen fish to native peoples as a substitute for banned river fish shows gross insensitivity to the wider cultural significance of food-gathering activities; the promised financial compensation for mercury poisoning was an unconscionably long time in coming.

Having looked at institutional contexts, we must now turn briefly to individual reactions. What is the meaning of environmental issues for the busy citizen in an industrial society? Environmental problems constitute a small proportion of the news items that flash by every day; major oil spills and other catastrophic events make headlines for a day or two, but most such problems (such as the passage of chlorinated compounds through the aquatic food chain) are quite complex and require serious and sustained attention if they are to be understood. There are real difficulties in attempting to incorporate our knowledge of them, together with a wide range of other considerations, into changed patterns of attitudes and behaviour.

Thus most persons will be content to trust university science researchers and regulatory authorities to manage environmental problems as they occur, without even wishing to become aware of such problems. Their real impact will be felt only indirectly in our everyday affairs at work and shopping. Greater expenses for pollution-control equipment will be passed along by producers and will appear as higher prices for goods and services. Some increased expenses, such as emission-control devices for automobiles, are quite evidently the outcome of environmental policies; the widespread practice of sabotaging the apparatus to improve gas mileage reveals the gap between individual and social benefit-cost ratios. Impact assessment requirements for large-scale developments can delay construction and threaten short-term employment. More stringent standards for hazardous substances may affect decisions on siting new mining and manufacturing plants, an especially serious matter for economically depressed areas with persistently high unemployment. Temporary bans on fishing, controversies over whether to spray New Brunswick forests against the spruce budworm, measures to reduce dust and gases in mines: all of these and many other questions have been accompanied by threats from large corporations to shut down operations that would, it is claimed, become uneconomic because of higher costs brought about by environmental protection.

What are individuals whose livelihood is at stake to do under these circumstances? Almost invariably spokespersons for the dominant institutional interests maintain that alleged environmental hazards have been either wildly exaggerated or completely unproved. Contradictory evidence from different scientific researchers is advanced. In many cases the problems, such as air pollution from automobiles, are spread over a wide area but the economic impact of mitigating them is concentrated in certain localities (Detroit or Oshawa). Sometimes the problem is exported entirely to another country, as is the potential pollution of Manitoba water by North Dakota irrigation schemes or the high salinity of Colorado River water when it crosses the us-Mexican border.

Individuals face plenty of threats to their well-being – poverty, discrimination, family break-up, illness – and plenty of opportunities – financial success, prestige and power, comfort, security. These threats and opportunities arise directly and immediately in everyday life. Most environmental concerns appear ambiguous, remote, or impossibly difficult to understand (when they are known at all) except to the relatively few people whose lives are now seriously affected by them.

At present the benefits of more rigorous environmental standards for most people tend to be confined to intangible quality-of-life measures, whereas the costs are expressed in far more tangible terms, such as jobs. This is the chief cause of any diminished sensitivity to environmental issues, for a feeling of improvement or deterioration in the quality of life is elusive and hard to measure. It is linked with the feeling that the relation between the individual and his or her surrounding environment has been enhanced or degraded. It is usually experienced indirectly rather than directly, as the contextual background (encompassing both physical environment and social relations) of daily activities; on it depends in large measure the degree of enjoyment derived from those activities.

Major changes in this contextual background affect our ranking of preferences and personal objectives, our awareness of sensations in our environment (sounds, colours, smells), and therefore the quality of the satisfactions we experience in work, play, and consuming. In transitional periods, when, for example, many people are moving from rural to urban environments, such contextual changes can lead to considerable ambiguity in personal experience. In our society one indicator of this ambiguity is the widespread use in advertising of background imagery derived from rural and wilderness settings; these settings, I think, tap older reservoirs of feeling through which individuals interpret the qualities of their new experiences, which are now oriented primarily toward the omnipresent consumer-goods displays in urban settings.

The Contextual Circle

In the preceding section I tried to show how the manifest politics of environmental issues emerges from the tension between established institutional forces and individual perceptions of well-being and self-interest. The resolution of this tension determines how environmental concerns will be understood and how they will be ranked in the range of social issues at any moment. But if changes in the contextual background of individual experiences affect in turn perceptions and judgments, then one must look beyond the level of manifest politics. The circularity of the process – contextual changes influencing individual preferences, resulting eventually in changed perceptions of the context – makes it especially difficult for social analysis.

One way of explaining this 'contextual circle' is as follows. The so-called mass consumption society that emerged in North America following the Second World War created not only greater quantities of consumer goods but also a new 'social world.' Individuals have been encouraged to abandon long-established practices (such as thrift and the production at home of such things as food and clothing) and to adopt different ones: rapid turnover of possessions, waste, credit buying, constant attention to the stimulus of the market-place, denigration of 'home-made' items. This changed general orientation affects the individual's sense of enjoyment, satisfaction, and well-being – in short, the ingredients that make up that elusive indicator known as the quality of life.[8] (This line of argument is worked out more fully in the next chapter.)

The behavioural orientation of a mass-consumption society encourages us to regard the natural environment instrumentally – as a means for supplying our wants. We see little intrinsic value in a relatively undisturbed natural landscape – its physical contours as well as its flora and fauna – and generally we wish to modify it as quickly as possible in order to make it yield those produced things we now prize so highly.

We recall sometimes that other people (the 'backward' or 'primitive' sort) took a different view. They also drew sustenance from their natural surroundings, but to them it had meaning or symbolic significance over and above its ability to supply their material wants. The land itself, its particular features, the flora and fauna it nourished, provided continuity for human cultures. It had 'always' been there, and groups hoped to bequeath it with undiminished abundance to succeeding generations. The animals especially were more than a resource: they too possessed 'spirits' and in this common dimension helped sustain the bonds of identification between humanity and its habitat that gave meaning to existence. In the nineteenth century, Chief Joseph of the Nez Percé told the European invaders on this continent, who were indiscriminately slaughtering the bison herds, that 'without the animals man would perish of a great loneliness of spirit.' They were unpersuaded.

Thomas Berger's pipeline inquiry report presented to us in the context of a major social policy issue a challenge based in part on re-affirmation of that older life-style. He investigated not only the more immediate issues of industrial development and native settlements in the north, such as alcoholism and family disintegration, but also the deeper structure of experience rooted in a special orientation to the natural environment. He quoted a native witness: 'Being an Indian means being able to understand and live with this world in a very special way. It means living with the land, with the animals, with the birds and fish, as though they were your sisters and brothers. It means saying the land is an old friend and an old friend your father knew, your grandfather knew, indeed your people always have known.'[9] And he recommended that southern Canadians take these expressions seriously when they decide how to introduce further industrial development in the north.

Many persons might regard this sentiment as a manoeuvre by native peoples to improve their bargaining position. Cash settlements for native land claims are simple and tidy – and specify terms that are readily comprehended by us. Although Berger made it quite clear that he was not urging southerners to adopt the native peoples' attitude toward the natural environment, even its presence in policy deliberations can be unsettling.

Does this point have any relevance outside the controversies about resource development in the north? Perhaps. Most people derive a deep sense of satisfaction from caring for others, and from being cared for in turn by them. This is expressed in our philosophical and religious tradition by the doctrine that a person should not be treated by others merely as a means to the realization of their objectives, but always also as a being of intrinsic worth, worthy of care and respect simply because he or she is part of the community of persons. Of course people are treated as means for the satisfaction of others, for extracting love, profit, and innumerable other resources. The traditional doctrine recognizes this but also teaches us to bridle our extractive impulses by reflecting on whether or not what we require of others on our own behalf is good for them as well. And our society today acknowledges, as a public responsibility, a mutual obligation for the welfare of all persons far higher than what prevailed not so very long ago.

Earlier cultures included both the land and other animals as well as humans in the 'community of beings' that grounded their sense of shared concern and responsibility. Our industrial culture, influenced by the idea that we have 'conquered' nature, discourages us from following their example. Indeed we cannot do so: our entire way of life is far too different. However, we should not take this to mean that we need not care at all about our relationship to the natural environment.

Today we do see the environment almost exclusively as a means for providing resources to satisfy our needs. But out of those resources we fashion the material goods that we use, and when we select from among such goods those that appeal to us, we are choosing those that we think express our own identity and personality, that reflect in part the qualities of our selves that we would like others to regard as worthy of respect. The connection between our concern for our own well-being and that of other persons and our relation to the natural environment is not immediate (as it was in earlier cultures). It is indirect, and it is concealed by the other connection we have made so important in our lives, namely the vital link between the sense of well-being and the increase of goods.

Should we attempt to connect more directly our sense of well-being – or our perception of the quality of life – and our relationship to the natural environment?[10] Does it make sense to speak, in terms appropriate to our industrial culture, of broadening our caring attitude to include the land and other natural entities as well as persons? Raising such questions carries no implication that the environment can or should cease to have vital economic significance to us, as the material basis for the satisfaction of needs. Of course it must continue to do so. But can it have a much greater, non-economic significance as well? In the next chapter I pursue these questions further.

8
CARING FOR THINGS

The 1970s will be remembered in Western nations as a period of 'energy crisis.' Rapid escalation in world prices for oil helped to inflict severe inflation on their economies, and panic afflicted the public over the prospect of 'running out of energy.' Characteristically, that panic subsided just as quickly when its proximate cause was removed, as pressures eased on energy supplies and prices. In the mean time governments had moved heaven and earth to re-establish their control over assured energy supplies. Demonstrating expertise in resource economics became the bureaucratic watchword of the day.

New, even minor disruptions would rekindle panic and insecurity. I noted in chapter 7 the paradox of affluence and insecurity and wish now to explore this point more fully. I wish to suggest that this insecurity has arisen because our consumer society gradually has eroded the social basis for the individual's development of a stable sense of well-being and personal identity. If this is indeed the case, then generalized insecurity about retaining our material affluence is a permanent condition in such a society, no matter what prodigies of future productivity our fecund science, technology, and industry are capable of.

I also want to explore a different way of addressing this condition, through looking not at supplies of goods, now and in the future, but rather at the ways in which those goods come to have meaning or significance for our lives. Specifically, I want to outline what may be called a 'conservation ethic,' based on the concept of caring, that might provide a practical moral foundation for a sense of well-being now lacking in consumer society. This effort parallels philosopher Albert Borgmann's exquisite reflections on what modern technology has done to the meaning of the 'world of things' that surrounds us.[1]

Life-style Change in the Consumer Society

There are many accounts of what is meant by the phrase 'consumer society.' As used here, it means a society in which most individuals have access to large numbers of goods; in which many goods have complex characteristics; in which the characteristics of goods change quickly and frequently; and in which an enormous number of 'messages' suggest to individuals what should be their personal objectives in their consumption activities.[2]

The consumer society is quite new: for all practical purposes it emerged only in the 1950s. Thus most people born in North America before 1945 can remember a quite different kind of ethos: a 'conserver society,' in which most people practised, probably not consciously, a 'conservation ethic.' They took pride in prolonging the useful life of their possessions through their skills in reusing and repairing them. For instance, I remember as a child carefully refolding the lunch bag I had carried to school so that I could take it home to use again. My father spent much time each evening in winter preparing the coal-burning stoves for the night so as to achieve maximum benefit from the right amount of fuel. Clothing, toys, and tools were repaired for as long as possible; as children we were admonished constantly not to 'waste' anything. These probably trivial examples illustrate a habit of mind that was widespread.

Some would explain such behaviour as a response to poverty or economic necessity: people practised this kind of conservation because they could not afford not to do so. We tend to find such 'straightforward' reasoning comforting nowadays, because it can express the bases of our behaviour in quantitative terms. But we should consider the matter more closely before accepting such a facile explanation.

The older conservationist behaviour was supported by the idea that waste was 'wrong,' or 'immoral.' This idea was often associated with formal religious teaching but sometimes presented as a non-religious, ethical principle. Obviously this principle was most meaningful to people who had to be frugal in their consumption patterns. But it had broader significance as well. I think that there is a close relationship between 'caring' about how we use material goods and caring about ourselves (self-respect) and other people. Surely, then, an adequate sense of personal satisfaction and well-being requires some kind of caring attitude of this sort.

The consumer society encourages us to discard things that are no longer 'fashionable', even if those things have many remaining useful and pleasing qualities. Yet as we consume things we 'invest' our own personality and feelings in them. In buying clothes or cars we believe that in part our choices 'say something' about ourselves to others whose approval and friendship we seek. As many people respond to more types of fashion trends, they must become indifferent to the things that they have and how they use them at any particular time, since they will soon be 'obsolete'. The personal feelings and inter-personal associations invested in their possessions are discarded along with the goods, to be replaced by a new set. The consumer society encourages us to regard not only material goods but our own states of feeling toward ourselves and others as easily disposable.

Individuals did not give up that older behaviour pattern, with its values of thrift and conservation, simply because more disposable income became available. In a short period following the Second World War, many North Americans increased quite dramatically their real incomes and thus their consumption of goods and services. But to me the cultural context that shapes our attitudes about using goods seems crucial – in this case, a far-too-rapid change in 'life-style models'. This development, rather than more material consumption per se, rapidly eroded the older values.

This was partly a matter of chance. The economic developments that made possible greater material consumption coincided with im-portant technological innovations in mass communications media. Television (and, to a lesser degree, improved colour photography in magazines) vastly increased individuals' daily exposure to the per-suasive images of material consumption employed in both adver-tising and the media content it sponsored. In addition the special qualities of its visual imagery made television much more influen-tial than radio. Psychological studies have shown that information or messages are conveyed far more effectively when associated with visual images, as opposed to being put simply into written or spoken form.[3]

During the same period, individuals were changing their daily ac-tivities. So-called time budget studies show in detail where the changes occurred. On average individuals spent less time on (for example) walking, reading, and eating meals; about half of this time was reallocated into watching television.[4] Both the amount of time spent each day watching television and the special effectiveness of visual imagery are significant. For individuals are now exposed every day to highly effective presentations of 'modern' life-styles – not only in advertisements, but also in the background settings of the programs themselves, for instance, the automobiles, homes, clothing, and other possessions owned by the characters.

Both direct messages in advertisements and indirect messages in background settings influence values, preferences, and behaviour. All media together (television, radio, billboards, magazines, newspapers, store displays, and so forth), present myriad 'cues' for individuals. The common underlying theme is the invitation to try something new, to change preferences and attitudes, with the suggestion that greater personal success or happiness will result. The unrecognized consequence is the simultaneous undermining of stable and readily identifiable indicators for personal well-being.

For instance, the stronger ethnic ties of older generations kept alive traditional customs of dress, cuisine, and popular entertainment; perpetuating these customs provided a stable reference-point for the sense of individual satisfaction. In contrast, the 'homogenized' popular culture of the consumer society continuously promotes new fashions in such matters, and rapid turnover of new styles does not allow individuals to achieve any depth of experience.

To take another example, a young person's choice of vocation was often a matter of careful consideration in middle- and lower-middle-class families, and as a result the person expected to derive much of her or his satisfaction in life from performing with skill the tasks of this vocation. At present, the overriding personal imperative is to maximize one's income, and individuals are constantly urged to re-educate themselves to qualify for different, higher-paying jobs. Cultural guidance once afforded different, clearly recognizable standards by which to measure achievements and to find satisfaction in them.

The decline in stable indicators of well-being probably increases ambiguity and confusion in the sense of personal satisfaction.[5] Without institutional guidance from outside the market-place, and bombarded daily with complex, every-changing symbols of success in the messages and cues that refer us always back to the market-place, individuals can only keep searching for the right life-style 'package' – and hope that it does not become obsolete before they have assembled it. Everyday life in the consumer society somewhat resembles a lottery.

Values and the Sense of Well-Being

In the type of market society that existed until the 1950s most families already depended for their livelihood on earning incomes through employment for wages, but the market-place itself, particularly consumer buying, was not the principle source for forming one's sense of well-being. Until the advent of the consumer society, the sense of well-being was formed primarily by cultural systems – values and customs that existed independent of economic determinations. Definitions of roles, codes of individual behaviour, and ideas about what represented 'worthy' accomplishments in life were derived from ethical postulates that had evolved largely in the context of formal religious teachings, whether or not actually expressed as such. The dominant social values rooted in those religious traditions incorporated a number of principles: caring for one's family, defined more or less extensively, directly rather than with the assistance of public institutions; employment in a trade or profession as itself a worthy accomplishment, apart from its particular monetary advantages; maintenance of established roles, for example, sex roles; continuity of family association; pride in self-reliance in a wide variety of life skills.

All this is not meant to portray a golden age by comparison with present relative degradation and iniquity. Quite the contrary. These earlier socialization patterns had regressive aspects that lent legitimacy to many injustices. Thus they are recalled here not as intrinsically worthy ideals (although they had many worthy aspects) but only to point out the former independence of well-being from *direct* determination by the market-place. Market-place cues are not appropriate guides for how we ought to act and make choices. What a market can do, with varying degrees of success, is to adjust supply and demand in response to a given set of preferences.[6] It should not be relied on to indicate what our preferences ought to be.

It is vitally important for us to begin to recognize this fundamental defect in our consumer society. It is equally important to devise a sensible way of remedying it. There is no turning back: no return to the 'good old days,' no reinstallation of 'traditional' values, is possible, for the social infrastructure that nourished them has disappeared. There are distinct advantages as well as disadvantages in the process of social change that led us from the older type of market society to the consumer society. It was not the material progress in that transition that gave rise to the problematic patterns I have described, but rather the far-too-rapid pace of the transition. There was insufficient time for value systems and cultural norms to adjust to economic changes and to exert some independent authority over the individual and social consequences of those changes. Values must possess some resilience and resistance to change if they are to be values at all; they need not and indeed should not be impervious to change, but they require time to uphold some continuity with the past while exerting their influence on a new social environment.

A Philosophy of Caring

A value or an ethical postulate is something that is regarded as being intrinsically worthy and good. Personal honesty, for example, is such a value that is widely shared in our society. When we say that a certain course of action is intrinsically good, we mean that it is to be followed no matter what the circumstances of the moment or the probable consequences of the action. This does not mean that we are entirely indifferent to the outcome: we believe that widespread commitment to personal honesty will result in a better society for everyone. But no value can be established by a utilitarian calculus, by adding up benefits and costs to discover whether or not they yield a net advantage. This is because our conception of benefits and costs itself is determined by the criteria we apply, that is, by the relative weights we assign to some types of action as opposed to others – in sum, by our definition of a 'good life.'

In simple terms this means that we do not and indeed cannot 'choose' our values in the same way that we choose our styles of clothing or automobiles. Some types of judgment are more fundamental than others, and different criteria must be brought to bear on the various levels in a hierarchy of judgments or choices. Most people recognize that their everyday choices reflect some sense of priorities in various possible courses of action, and in commonsense terms such schedules of priorities represent an operative system of values.

Liberal-democratic societies have a public stance toward values that differs from most other societies and from their own past histories. In this stance, values are said to be largely a matter of individual judgment, except in certain well-defined areas. This contrasts with the more common pattern, where behavioural codes are more rigidly ordained and enforced by laws and public opinion, even in such matters as dress and appearance. This recent development coincides with, and is an essential aspect of, the consumer society, which deliberately encourages individuals to experiment with their tastes and preferences.

Many of the values held by preceding generations are incompatible with the consumer society's orientation. For instance, the level of indulgence in credit buying that is promoted by businesses, banking institutions, and governments today would horrify earlier ages; yet our economic 'prosperity' is unthinkable without it, given existing institutional arrangements. (In Canada bank loans for purchases of large consumer durables such as automobiles were uncommon before the mid-1950s.) Different social structures employ quite different mechanisms for inculcating a code of responsible behaviour in individuals. Today we rely on individuals to retain enough common sense to remain financially solvent amid constant blandishments to indulge themselves with their credit cards. Most people have managed so far, but the level of current consumer indebtedness creeps slowly upward.

Sometime in the future, however, the consumer society could shift into a second, more 'mature' phase. In this second phase, market-place indicators of performance still will be very important, both for society as a whole and for most individuals, but their significance for us could change.[7] The first phase of the consumer society has been marked by a 'turning outward' of individuals toward their social environment generally as the source of cues for approved behaviour, conceptions of personal identity and self-respect, and life-styles. As we have seen, this represents a departure from the traditional frameworks for the value systems that had once generated those cues, which had been based in extended family and community (ethnic) associations. A second, mature phase of the consumer society – if it were to come into being – would be marked by a reverse development, a 'turning inward.' This would not be a mechanical reversal back toward those traditional frameworks: they have disappeared (or are in the process of doing so). This restructuring of value frameworks would result in a more diffuse, heterogeneous, and individualized pattern by comparison with those in the first phase.[8]

Such a new turning inward must be distinguished from other recent, superficially similar developments – namely, some new 'religious' cults and the personal therapy industry. Most of the former are rooted in the search for an authoritarian group identity that is the precise opposite of personal identity, since they depend in fact on the destruction of personal identity. The latter is usually more an expression of the first phase of the consumer society than its transcendence: individuals shop around for therapy services much as one might canvass the offerings of fast-food outlets. What both lack is any attempt to integrate personal development with broader social concerns. This is precisely what earlier value systems, rooted in the traditional frameworks mentioned above, strived to do. A restructuring of value systems in the second phase of the consumer society should be founded on a similar integration of personal and social dimensions.

The philosophy of caring provides an excellent framework for this purpose.[9] It has its source and strength in the interpersonal relationships on which the bonds of extended families and traditional communities are founded. In this respect it draws on some of the most stable and enduring wellsprings known for responsible individual development. But it is also amenable to extension and reformulation in the light of contemporary experience, including a practical dimension that is relevant to public policy issues.[10]

The philosophy of caring has two essential features: (1) caring gives one an ordering of priorities; (2) caring gives one a sense of 'being in place' or 'being at home' in the world. Together these features provide the foundations for a stable sense of well-being. Caring is commonly regarded as involving primarily a relation to other persons, although we also extend our caring at least as far as other sentient beings, notably animals. However, it is actually broader than this: we can care for anything that we regard as having intrinsic value. Thus we can and do care about ideals, ideas, and artistic accomplishments; about reputations, honour, and integrity; about the future; about unfulfilled potentialities; and so on.

Since its domain is so broad, caring is liable to lose all clearly identifiable characteristics and to become indistinguishable from simple 'concern' or 'interest.' We can pin down its unique properties in the following way. Caring means concern for the 'other' (person, ideal, object) according to its own principle of being or development. The essence of caring, therefore, is not just our own state of concern for the other, but a specific form of concern, namely, for the intrinsic integrity of the other.

The best example of caring in this sense is the relation between parent and child. The everyday expression of parental caring is in providing the best possible external environment, according to particular cultural norms: emotional bonds, nutrition, role models, education, and so forth. At a deeper level, however, we look for something more than the production of a well-nourished, well-educated representative of a cultural type; we look for expressions of individuality, especially capacity for individual judgment. The kind of concern that makes this development possible must allow the other sufficient space for exercising faculties of judgment, including willingness to support the other if (and especially when) we 'know' he or she is making a wrong choice. Thus caring must restrain its concern, when this would conflict with the other's requirements for the autonomy that is a necessary part of its individuality.

As an example of our caring for things or objects we might think of a family heirloom. The association with memories of other persons that are 'carried' by the object makes up much of its value for us, and it cannot be replaced by another object that happens to have identical physical properties. These associations become part of the object itself, so that it is possible to regard doing certain things to or with it as inappropriate (for example, replacing the picture in a frame). Later I shall suggest that we can extend this concept and that we can care for objects in the absence of association with memories of other persons.

When we care for 'abstractions,' such as ideals, we have regard not only for our public demonstrations of adherence to them but also for whether our everyday actions conform with the 'spirit' as well as the 'letter' of our ideals. In other words, the ideals make demands of their own, stemming from such factors as logical consistency or historical associations, that continuously challenge our professed concern for them. For example, the ideal of equality of treatment for all persons has coexisted in ongoing tension with different social practices (such as discrimination based on race or gender), which come under criticism for being – from a new perspective – inconsistent with the ideal. A powerful ideal has an inner logic of development of its own, and our caring for it is in one sense precisely what allows the ideal's own development to take place.

Caring thus supplies what is most basic to any value system: a clear view of priorities and of individual responsibility. Caring ought not to occur as only an expression of the interests of the one who professes care; on the contrary, it should always consider the 'standpoint' of the other. The state of being or development of the other is (as mentioned earlier) the central reference for caring and determines what is appropriate action on the part of one who cares. Caring means placing the highest priority on the other's realization of the appropriate state of being or development.

Through caring and being cared for we achieve a sense of being in place or being at home in the world. When we care for another in the way described above, we do so on the basis of a judgment about what is most appropriate for the being or development of the other at a given point in time and space. In other words, we judge the appropriateness of our action by how it affects the relation of the other to its 'environment.' This type of judgment presupposes willingness to take sufficient time and patience to understand the situation of the other in depth and to reflect on the tensions and possibilities that characterize any situation before choosing a course of action.

Being in place, like the concept of stability, does not entail rigidity or the notion of a pre-established order to which persons and things must 'conform.' It is applicable to a dynamic, changing environment as well as to one that is relatively static. Being in place refers essentially to some sense of coherence in the overall scheme of things, to a perception of a meaningful network of associations or relationships where each component part has some unique properties that are valued as its contribution to the overall significance of the whole.

Through our own expressions of caring we reveal at the same time our own need for the emergence of caring behaviour in other persons. Caring orients others toward ourselves in reciprocal movement, binding us and them in a network of associations. So long as these bonds are true expressions of caring they will not be fetters or restrictions, but rather preconditions for our own freedom to develop our individuality. For our individuality can never result from a mere absence of external control; without a complementary attention to the needs of others it can easily degenerate into tyranny. A network of reciprocal caring relationships gives to each participant a sense of being in his or her own place in the world.

In our society today we believe that we have a reasonably effective public commitment to the philosophy of caring as it applies to persons. We express our commitment less and less in traditional forms, through the maintenance of extended families and communities, and more in terms of social welfare policies. We believe that we have assigned sufficiently clear mandates to public agencies to ensure that no one is denied access to the basic material necessities of existence. What is mainly lacking in these arrangements, however, by contrast with traditional ones, is any personal involvement in the process of caring for others. Thus, although our bureaucratic forms of caring undoubtedly help those who depend on them, they do not incorporate the two essential features of caring, namely, the ordering of priorities resulting from a direct relation with the other and a sense of being in place in a network of caring relationships.

Our society has split the process of caring that was united in traditional socialization networks. Caring for others outside the domain of the nuclear family, in terms of basic needs, has been relegated increasingly to public agencies. At the same time the formation of a sense of personal identity and well-being has been detached from the network of caring relationships and routed instead through the market-place – which, I have suggested, cannot successfully perform this function.

Now I should like to extend the concept of caring to the domain of things. I will discuss two examples of conservation-as-caring to illustrate these features: using things in accordance with the priorities established by the qualities of the things themselves; and preserving and prolonging the useful life of things, instead of replacing them in obedience to the whims of fashion, in order to establish a 'relationship' with objects that helps to form the sense of being in place.

We know that we do not make the best use of the qualities of fossil fuels when we burn them to heat our buildings and generate electricity. We can see a 'hierarchy of qualities' in the substance itself (petroleum in this case) that ought to affect our choice of the uses to which we put it, at least more than it does now. Those qualities that yield petrochemical products are more unique and more characteristic than those that produce combustion. Further, the tremendous inefficiencies at all stages in the process of (for example) electrical heating of homes through oil-fired generation stations waste most of the combustible properties themselves. Our caring for the object in this case would mean allowing its intrinsic hierarchy of qualities to influence more the uses to which it is applied.

With family heirlooms we usually take special care; but I believe that we can and should be more caring with the ordinary range of objects, notably our personal possessions, that we encounter in daily life.[11] Many kinds of things that are not mass-produced have special qualities – for example, the grain in wood – that lend the thing a uniqueness and character of its own. But even mass-produced objects can acquire a 'character' if they are given the time necessary to do so, instead of being replaced at the first available opportunity, by virtue of their 'being there' during an extended period in which we have derived pleasure from using them. In many ways the thing itself can undergo a process of 'development' as an aesthetic object; for example, the finish on a piece of furniture can develop a patina with special qualities all its own.

Our caring for objects can contribute to a feeling of being in place, in that we associate ourselves with things that themselves have a 'history,' that is, a tradition of development of their own unique qualities or of associations in memory with activities and events that have been important to us. Being in place means being accorded the treatment appropriate for the unique qualities of the entity. We have achieved a proper set of priorities for our own demands on the earth's resources when we structure those demands in such a way that, as much as possible, they respect the intrinsic hierarchy of qualities in those resources and, similarly, when we structure our uses and care of things in such a way that we allow them the time to develop their full potentialities as both useful and aesthetic objects. The more we do so, the richer is the network of meaningful associations that we allow to emerge in the world around us. And the richer that network is, the more possibilities there are for feeling 'in place' in the world and for constructing a stable sense of well-being.

Albert Borgmann uses a different but complementary approach in contrasting 'commodities' with 'focal things.' Commodities, which are the goods surrounding us in stores and advertisements, are the products of modern technologies; they are 'abstract': in emerging from industrial production processes they present themselves to us as free from local and historical associations. Focal things are 'deep,' showing themselves to us with so many concrete and subtle qualities that they defy description: 'A thing is deep if all or most of its physically discernible features are finally significant.' Borgmann's own prime example of a focal thing is wilderness.[12]

In broad terms, conservation-as-caring can guide a reorientation of behaviour away from 'extensive' forms of experience, where we are concerned primarily with the range of goods and activities, toward 'intensive' forms, where we are concerned primarily with the depth and fullness of our associations with persons and things. The intensive mode that is characteristic of caring encourages and supports the 'turning inward,' in the formation of personal identity, that would signal the beginning of a mature phase of the consumer society.

The Uses of Caring

It has been said that 'conservation is not an end in itself, but instead a means toward furthering economic and social goals that involve resource use.'[13] Certainly conservation is a means of extending the useful life of resources and of extracting greater tangible benefits from them by eliminating unnecessary waste. In my view, however, this is too narrowly utilitarian an interpretation.

I propose that in the consumer society we should define 'standard of living' not only by quantitative indicators (such as per-capita energy consumption) but also by the changing network of qualitative, symbolic associations that link images of happiness with goods and services. However, these symbolic associations are often ambiguous and confusing, and so greater material affluence does not firmly increase the sense of well-being in our society as a whole.[14]

Eventually we should try to formulate for ourselves more stable, personal indicators of satisfaction and well-being. A philosophy of caring can help bring this about. Most people derive deep satisfaction from caring for others and from being cared for in turn by them. And our society acknowledges as public responsibility an obligation in this regard, even if often cast in impersonal, bureaucratic forms, far greater than was the case in earlier times.

In our fascination with the seductive promises of the consumer society, with its rapid turnover of fashions and preferences, we have forgotten that this caring attitude once extended to our use of nature's resources as well. Out of those resources we make and choose the things that express in part our own identity and personality and that reflect the qualities of our selves that we would like others to regard as being worthy of respect. These are, I suggest, the deepest and the most stable and enduring sources of the sense of satisfaction, well-being, and quality of life.

9
THE MISINFORMATION SOCIETY

I n a 1981 report for the government of Canada, *The Information Revolution and Its Implications for Canada*, we read: 'Like the industrial revolution, the information revolution is unavoidable. Consequently, the objectives of public policy should be not to prevent the revolution from occurring, but rather to turn it to our advantage.'[1] The mention of public policy signals a new phase in technocratic thinking, that mode of thought which claims that prevailing institutions and values must adapt to new technologies.

This theme brings us back full circle to our starting-point in chapter 2: the effects, on societies and individuals, of the immense growth in the stock of technical knowledge during modern times. We encounter also another theme that ran through much of part I: the strong undercurrent of fatalism resulting from the notion of technological imperatives. And yet, as I shall try to show here, dissecting the concept of the information society brings its reward. The fatalism dissolves, and we are left with the inescapable duty and necessity of making choices, through public policies responsive to democratic authority, based on fundamental values such as justice, equity, and fairness.

The theorists of the information society tell us that our social relations must be adapted to the specifications of advanced technologies. Another recent Canadian government report states that 'the advent of microelectronics is rapidly and irreversibly leading to a major and fundamental transformation of western society.'[2] In past times the inevitability or necessity allegedly inherent in technological innovation was presumed to have a direct, unmediated effect on social relations via decisions made in the market-place, which were thought to make government intervention unnecessary and indeed counter-productive. In the current phase, public policy and government action are supposed to serve historical inevitability by facilitating a favourable social response to it.

Two quite different sets of circumstances have given rise to this new phase. First, the rate of technical innovation and turnover has accelerated; together with the intensity of international competition this means that societies must respond much more quickly than they did in the past, and the mission of public policy is to provide some 'grease' to ensure faster response. Second, some interest groups are now much better able to defend themselves by protecting their income, status, and influence against innovations that threaten to erode their relative advantages.

The enhanced ability of social groups to articulate their interests – and to require governments to protect those interests – places an important intervening variable between technological innovation (operating through the economy) and social relations. Public policy must seek to persuade us to acquiesce in what we can no longer be forced to accept, at least not without protracted struggle. And that is just the point: if the innovating forces must triumph in the end, they will have achieved only a Phyrric victory, for the economic advantages of early entry will have been lost, and society will drift further and further away from 'the action' as each successive wave of innovation rolls in.

The concepts of 'information revolution,' 'information economy,' and 'information society' constitute an important new stage in modern technocratic thinking. They perfectly represent this tradition. They enable us to see clearly what role public policy is thought to have in the interaction between technology and society – namely, to 'soften up' public opinion so that a compliant social response to a new technology may be delivered. For the propagators of these concepts the main objective in this case, as it is in technocratic thinking generally, is to attempt to persuade us that we are free to choose only the timing of our submission.

The effort at persuasion introduces a nice circularity into the process. If we can be cajoled into believing that some future state is inevitable, and further to alter our behaviour in order to conform to its anticipated requirements, the end result will be retrospective proof of the prediction's accuracy. There are five principal steps: (1) *Analysis* develops a conceptual model, namely, the concept of the 'information society,' whose objective is to influence (2) *policy* initiatives that will create favourable conditions for shaping a (3) *social response* that over time will result in changed social behaviour and new (4) *behaviour patterns* that resemble those originally predicted as desirable in the (5) *analysis* itself, thus confirming the model's predictions about what was 'inevitable.'

In times past when many thought that it was salutary for society to be utterly at the mercy of the market-place's allocative mechanisms and that 'interference' by public authority was to be avoided, the apparent 'necessity' in the process of social change required no further justification. Public policy today, however, as the explicit voice of public authority, abdicates its responsibility and loses it raison d'être when it limits itself to the 'recognition of necessity.' For strictly speaking, there is no necessity in social events; rather, they represent the outcomes of individual and collective choices (including both conscious and unconscious motivations) that rest ultimately on fundamental values. From this standpoint, public policy discussions should clarify the full range of choices and their possible effects on values, so that citizens can make enlightened decisions and choices for the future.

I will examine the information society in the context of my own evaluative standpoint, summarized briefly here, to which I will return in the concluding section. It has three major features. First, increases in the stock of information are counterbalanced by an equally large growth in misinformation and, in many cases, by deliberately constructed batches of disinformation. Second, inadequacies in basic literacy leave some citizens unable to use information in making informed judgments on social and political issues. Third, even if powerful pressures are exerted on industrial societies to adopt new technologies, given their integration into an international economic structure, these societies can and should resist the notion that they must adapt to the new environment in any predetermined way. The mode of adaptation is not fixed in advance but can be made responsive to reflective processes, through which societies retain a measure of freedom from necessity and of freedom of choice based on the autonomy of value systems.

Evolution of an Idea

The 'information society' and its associated notions evolved in a three-stage process during the past twenty years or so: from the 'technological society' to the 'knowledge society' and/or 'service society' to the 'information society.' The first two stages have been vetted in the preceding chapters, and in the present chapter we shall see where this is all supposed to lead.

In 1979 a report (*The Information Society*) prepared for the government of Canada offered the following definition: 'An Information Society is a set of social relationships based on an Information Economy. In turn, the Information Economy exists whenever over 50 per cent of the Gross National Product belongs within the broad information sector.'[3] In a very short time the concept of an information society has received considerable attention. How did it arise?

Daniel Bell's *The Coming of Post-Industrial Society* (1973) paved the way for the concept of an information society. Bell had relied heavily on some statistical evidence (from studies sponsored by the Organization for Economic Cooperation and Development [OECD] and other sources) to argue the growing preponderance of scientific and technical knowledge in industrialized economies. Subsequently there appeared an elaborate study, *The Information Economy* (1977), prepared by Marc Uri Porat for the US Office of Telecommunications, on which many later works have rested their case for the existence of the information economy.[4] 'The information economy' is the mainstay for the ensemble of social effects said to make up the information society.

Bell gave five distinguishing characteristics for post-industrial society:[5] (1) in the economic sector: the change from a goods-producing to a service economy; (2) in occupational distribution: the pre-eminence of the professional and technical class; (3) in axial principle: the centrality of theoretical knowledge as the source of innovation and of policy formation for the society; (4) in future orientation: the control of technology and technological assessment; and (5) in decision-making: the creation of a new 'intellectual technology.' Let us examine these claims, especially the first two.

The traditional classifications in the US Department of Labor statistics used by Bell and the percentage of the work-force in each category are shown (rounded) in Table 1.

Table 1
US Work-force by Category (percentage)

	1900	1960	1974
White-collar workers	17.5	42.0	48.5
Manual workers	36.0	37.5	35.0
Service workers	9.0	12.5	13.0
Farm workers	37.5	8.0	2.0

When these categories are re-analysed into just two sectors, goods-producing and services-producing, the figures for 1968 are: goods, 36 per cent; services, 64 per cent. In this far more simplified stratification, the actual composition of the two, especially the services-producing, is crucial. The services sector includes the following: transportation and utilities, 5.5 per cent; trade (wholesale and retail), 20.5 per cent; finance, insurance, and real estate, 4.5 per cent; services, 18.5 per cent; government, 14.5 per cent. Services are composed of personal (laundries, garages, hairdressing, and the like), professional (lawyers, doctors, and accountants), and business (office equipment, cleaning, and so on). The goods-producing sector includes only those directly employed in mining, construction, manufacturing, agriculture, forestry, and fisheries.

The heterogeneous character of the services sector should give one pause at the outset. First, replacing the white collar – manual labour distinction with the services – goods one can be misleading, for the two are not symmetrical (that is, white collar and services are not identical). Second, and more important, a large proportion of the services sector is a necessary and integrated part of goods-producing activities especially in transportation and utilities, but also in part of wholesale and retail trade, government, and business services as well. To some extent the inflated services sector reflects only the greater internal complexity of the goods-producing sector itself, which requires more infrastructural support now than it did earlier. In short, the goods – services distinction is a conceptual dichotomy, not a simple reflection of economic activity; one must be careful not to make too much of it.

Second, there is the alleged 'pre-eminence' of the professional and technical occupations in the economy as a whole. Included in the white-collar category, their proportion increased from 4.3 per cent in 1900 to 10.8 per cent in 1960 to 14.4 per cent in 1974. Who are they? For the United States in 1975, the breakdown was as follows: scientific and engineering (including social scientists), 15 per cent, of whom three-quarters were engineers; technicians (excluding medical and dental), 11 per cent; medical and health professionals, 17 per cent; teachers, 23 per cent, of whom three-quarters were elementary and secondary teachers; and general, 34 per cent (accountants, lawyers, media personnel, architects, librarians, clergymen, social workers, and so on).

What conclusions can be drawn from the data? The more traditional categorization (white-collar, manual, and so forth) shows in fact the remarkable stability of the 'manual' sector throughout the twentieth century. The principal redistributional shift has been the precipitous decline in farm workers, redistributed almost entirely into the while-collar sector. Although the white-collar sector is now numerically predominant, nothing in the numbers implies qualitative change in social influence. As Bell notes, traditional agrarian societies also have large services sectors – for example, household servants, made up of low-status occupations. The services sector today includes, as well as the high-status professions, a large proportion of low-status jobs in retail sales, clerical-typist positions, minor bureaucratic functions, and the like.

Bell says very little about this matter because point 2 is the real heart of his analysis: the professional and technical 'elite' of the service sector is 'pre-eminent' in our 'new kind of society.' He says: 'The central occupational category in the society today is the professional and technical.'[6] Even if we limit ourselves to his own framework for analysis, however, it is difficult to see why this is supposed to be so. First, the breakdown presented above shows clearly that this collection of professions is by no means a homogenous social entity with, even potentially, a sense of self-consciousness as a group and thus a distinctive social interest. The category itself is composed of sharply divided strata in terms of self-identity and perceived status differentiation; it lumps together the high-status professional 'elites' (doctors, lawyers, accountants, engineers, architects) along with teachers, technicians, nurses, social workers, and so forth.

Second, each of these two basic divisions seems to have much more in common, in income and social status, with those in other categories than with each other. For example, the professional elites have much in common with the stratum of corporate and government-sector managers and the more successful small proprietors, who are included in a separate occupational category. There is little, if any, evidence (Bell presents none) to suggest, as his scheme does in moving from point 2 to points 3–5, that the professional-technical group as a whole, based on what Bell calls its ability to use 'intellectual technology' (a fancy name for systems analysis, organizational theory, and the like), increasingly directs social change through policy formation, or even seeks to do so.

Bell's analysis is a classic case of special pleading. Bell highlights the pre-eminence of the professional-technical group by pointing to the dramatic rate of increase in this sector relative to others. For the 1958–74 period there was a 77.5 per cent increase, as opposed to a 55 per cent increase for white-collar workers as a whole. Nonetheless, the clerical sector grew by 65 per cent in the same period! There are also enough possible anomalies in this particular period, including the deliberate channelling of resources into education, space research, and military expansion, to induce caution. In any case, the high-lighting is achieved by segregating occupational groups that in reality have strong affinities.

The ultimate conclusion is as shaky as the analytical premises on which it is founded. For Bell, the distinguishing characteristics of post-industrial society signal 'the emergence of a new kind of society,' and, as in all such occurrences, this one 'brings into question the distributions of wealth, power, and status that are central to any society.'[7] In post-industrial society knowledge has emerged alongside property to constitute the two 'axes of stratification' for social relations. On the evidence submitted, this contention appears implausible. Occupational categories are useful for keeping statistical records but otherwise are rather arbitrary; one cannot concoct a social theory out of such ingredients alone, which is what Bell sought to do.

The Information Economy

All major commentaries on the information economy rely on Porat's path-breaking 1977 study. This work concluded that 46 per cent of the American gross national product (GNP) could be classified as information activity, and 53 per cent of all income as income earned by information workers. (The data go back mostly to 1967). Porat employed the following basic definition: 'Information is data that have been organized and communicated. The information activity includes all resources consumed in producing, processing and distributing information goods and services.' It is composed of six subsidiary types of activity: (1) information generation or creation; (2) information capture, or the channelling of information; (3) information transformation; (4) information processing (at the receiving end); (5) information storage; and (6) information retrieval.

The principal working hypothesis is that information activity is not an independent sector in the traditional sense, such as manufacturing is, but rather is something that cuts across all sectors. Thus the information component of all types of economic activity must be segregated and the results combined to provide an overall picture. Parenthetically Porat concedes that a similar operation could be performed with regard to educational activity, for example, since most types of economic activity have an educational or learning component. His type of approach does not exclude others that employ similarly broad or 'synthetic' concepts. This important qualification, not surprisingly, does not reappear in the policy literature that is otherwise dependent on Porat's scheme and would convert Porat's purely conceptual exercise into a statement about a 'new kind of society' that supposedly now exists.

When reshuffling of the information component of occupations is done, there are six elements in Porat's schema: a primary information sector, two secondary information sectors, and three non-information sectors. (1) The primary information sector is a private-market sector, including all of the computer and telecommunications industry, finance and insurance, media, and private education, as well as varying percentages of other industries. (2) The secondary information sector contains (a) public bureaucracy; and (b) private bureaucracy, including all 'information support' activities in large organizations. (3) The non-information sectors are (a) households; (b) the private productive sector; and (c) the public productive sector (for example, government-owned corporations). The primary information sector accounts for 25 per cent of GNP, and the secondary, for 21 per cent, giving a total of 46 per cent.

The proportion of information workers in the total labour population is classified by a three-part typology. The first part consists of knowledge producers (engineers, lawyers, most specialist occupations) and knowledge distributors, primarily teachers; the second, of knowledge users, including, in one sub-category, managers, ad-

Table 2
Classification of Information Work

Information producers
    A Scientific and technical: natural scientists, engineers, social scientists
    B Market specialists: brokers, buyers, insurance agents
    C Information gatherers: surveyors, inspectors
    D Consultative services: architects, planners, dieticians, accountants, lawyers, designers
    E Other: authors, composers

Information processors
    A Administrative/managerial: judges, office managers, administrators
    B Process control: supervisors, foremen
    C Clerical: typists, clerks, bookkeepers, receptionists

Information distributors
    A Educators: teachers (at all levels)
    B Communications workers: journalists, announcers, directors, producers

Information infrastructure
    A Information machines: office machine operators, printers and associated trades, a/v equipment operators
    B Postal and telecommunications workers

Source: Report on Economic Analysis of Information Activities (OECD)

ministrators, and bureaucrats and, in another, clerical and office staff; and the third, of direct operators of information-processing machines. By an elaborate segregation of activities in industries, Porat arrived at the figure of 53 per cent as the share of total income earned by information workers.

An appendix to the government of Canada's 1979 report on the 'information revolution' offers an overview of the major classifications and occupational types in what is called information work, taken from an OECD study, *Report on Economic Analysis of Information Activities* (see Table 2).

Two general issues arise immediately. First, there is a lack of correlation between the size of the information sectors in national economies and overall economic performance. The United States leads the way, in terms of size, followed by Canada and the United Kingdom; but West Germany is significantly lower, and Japan is lowest of all. This is almost certainly related to productivity figures.

During the past decade industrial productivity in the United States grew 90 per cent, whereas office productivity grew only 4 per cent; since so much of the information sector is office work, the report concedes that 'low growth in productivity may well have contributed to an expansion in information employment.'[8] If this is part of an 'information revolution,' something seems amiss, for it sounds a good deal more like a counter-revolution.

Second, much of what was said above about the service sector applies here as well. The information economy is a mixed bag of occupations; whether we see any unifying ingredient depends very much on our tolerance for terminological laxity. In any event the service and information sectors are the same cat, with only slightly different stripes: the same report tells us that in 1971 in Canada 76 per cent of information workers belonged to the service sector.

Relabelling is a perfectly legitimate undertaking for social analysts; very little under the Sun is new, and fresh understanding often is derived from rearranging familiar facts to fit another paradigm. Exercises such as Porat's, and speculative treatises such as Bell's, challenge other ways of thinking about the contemporary phase of industrial societies; even if one cannot accept them, one can appreciate the testing of accepted approaches that they inspire.

What Is an Information Society?

It is a different matter altogether when people attempt to compose marching music out of these scattered notes. The 1979 Canadian government report *The Information Society* states boldly: 'It is reasonable to assume that the Information Society is now as inevitable for the OECD countries as puberty is for an adolescent.' It further warns us to eschew reliance on either market forces or uncoordinated public policy and urges the government to adopt a 'concerted and comprehensive information policy.' The 1981 report *The Information Revolution* concurs: 'The social and economic impact of the information revolution could be as profound as that of the industrial revolution. Many industrialized countries recognize this fact, as well as the need for comprehensive approaches to policy in order to deal effectively with the widespread changes expected to result from pervasive application of these new technologies.'[9]

But before we leap on this bandwagon, let us pose a few unpleasant questions. We can easily grant that our economies now depend on a rapidly increasing and quickly circulating stock of data (that is, specialized knowledge) for *specific* purposes – building machinery, growing crops, producing entertainment, perpetrating crimes, conducting covert operations, and, above all, launching total war. But when we sum it all up, and consider the general relation between knowledge and the uses to which it is put, and by whom, what is the result?

The answer given below is: the 'information society' itself is a mythical creature. No such beast exists or is about to emerge, at least not under present conditions. Quite the contrary: in seeking to answer the question posed above, we are driven to the conclusion that, in some respects and in some places (particularly the United States), we are witnessing the emergence of its polar opposite, the misinformation society.

To avoid misunderstandings I wish to state explicitly that I accept the contentions that our advanced industrial economy rests on an increasingly rich information base and that the 'information component' of the economy, and thus the proportion of 'information workers' (both based on the Porat definition), are steadily growing and now account for over half of all economic activity, in the United States at least. And yet I contend that, in the absence of other essential conditions, this does not constitute anything that sensibly may be called an 'information society,' no matter how great is the information component in the economy. In other words, I take issue with what I regard as the illicit jump from the information economy (a rational and defensible concept) to the information society (in its present form, an illogical notion).

The reason is that the concept of an information society is a 'rational' notion only under certain conditions. There are two chief conditions. The first is that the great majority of the population should be in process of becoming increasingly 'knowledgeable,' through access to, and use of, the overall information treasure-house. The second is that this general use of enhanced information sources should measurably improve over time the citizen's capacity for informed judgment and, moreover, that this improved judgment should be brought to bear on the fundamental political issues of the day. In the absence of these conditions, I maintain, the mere existence and availability of vast new information stores is irrelevant, so far as the quality of social and political life is concerned, and the emphasis on their technical qualities alone (for example, the size, interrelations, and speed of access to massive electronic databases) is only a curious fetish.

These propositions will in a moment appear less outrageous than they do at first glance. No one can doubt that specialists can and do use new information to do new things of all sorts; when the process of systematically searching for new knowledge and applying it to practical ends is incorporated throughout an economy, we can speak of an information economy. But as we have already seen, the tradition of technocratic thinking wishes to go well beyond this straightforward observation: the argument is that qualitative change (for the better, of course) in social relations generally will be another outcome of this process. And this tradition suggests that when regular use of steadily growing knowledge is institutionalized, an 'information society' results.

However, at the very same time when an information economy is coming into being, other changes in society (or at least in some societies) may be eroding ordinary citizens' abilities to employ richer knowledge sources to make better-informed judgments on social and political issues. I have three kinds of abilities in mind – basic literacy, ordinary knowledge about the social and political world, and information processing.

The technological fetishists among us rejoice in the daily innovations in information delivery through electronic means. Much less attention is paid to a simple question: how many and what kinds of 'ordinary citizens' are capable of using this information? It is my contention that the elementary basis for using knowledge in informed judgment in everyday life is basic literacy, the capacity to understand and use ordinary, non-technical language as well as basic mathematical operations: the old-fashioned 'three Rs.' Many elaborate studies have documented the abysmally poor state of basic literacy in broad sections of the US population. At least one-third of adults cannot read at a level adequate to comprehend survival information, such as warning labels on products, or to ascertain whether their paycheques have been properly computed.[10]

Other surveys have sought to measure the average citizen's knowledge of current events both at home and abroad, such as the identity of prominent political figures and the nature of major events reported in the mass media. Results here are equally dismal, showing among other things that much of the vast information stream flows past many individuals unobserved and untapped.

Finally, there is increasing use of visually oriented media of communication, especially television, as well as the growing predominance of visual imagery for communicating messages, such as in advertising and signposts. This stands in contrast to the relative decline in reading and in the use of print-based information. Information, including highly technical material, can be communicated well by graphical means – and in many cases this may be a superior form of communication. However, much of our knowledge will always involve manipulation of words and language; even among those with basic literacy, therefore, there is a decreasing exercise for this facility, which over time will result in diminished capacity. Moreover, the most important aspects of social and political life require amicable mutual understanding with our fellow citizens, in the absence of which the tools of violence are often employed. It seems to me that, for the foreseeable future, we must rely primarily on words, not visual images, for our attempts to reach such an understanding both at home and abroad.

The Perils of 'Data Flak'

It is no accident that in many economically advanced democratic nations politics is tending to become more of an elaborate exercise in staged image management and less of a meaningful conceptual dialogue.[11] Current technology can offer politicians a second-by-second continuous readout, in graphs, bar charts, and numbers, of responses by selected audiences to their speeches (the audience members hold electronic response mechanisms in their laps). The politicians' 'handlers' then can gauge exactly which words, facial expressions, body gestures, and language tone are correlated with positive and negative reactions and make the necessary adjustments.[12] The carefully staged appearances of Oliver North before a congressional committee themselves caused huge swings in public opinion on us aid to the anti-Sandinista forces in Nicaragua.

Examples abound. What is at stake is by no means lack of information for the electorate. On the contrary, information is abundant, particularly via the print media, so long as one has the literacy skills and the willingness to find and digest it. However, image management and other techniques give rise to an equally impressive quantity of misinformation, disinformation, and what might be called – borrowing from the strategy of anti-aircraft defence – 'data flak.' As the sum total of accumulated information/misinformation grows, so also there arises the need for skilled piloting to shepherd the precious cargo of genuine knowledge and wisdom through the intense barrages of data flak. To change the metaphor, the abundant data flow carries a great deal of mischievous flotsam and jetsam; elaborate filtering is called for, but the requisite technologies are relatively under-developed.

The paradox of the so-called information society is this: on the great issues of society and politics, the role of knowledge in the composition of informed judgment very well may decline in proportion to the increase in available information.

In conclusion, the notions of information society and information technology, at least in their present form, show the impoverished state of technocratic thinking. Erected on flimsy conceptual foundations, composed of hastily recycled terminology, and motivated solely by the conviction that the show must go on, they offer us the old routine: a new technology demands a response from us that is appropriate to *its* essence and modes of action. Since little can be specified about the larger significance of the so-called information society, the actual message can be stated in stark simplicity: whatever is happening is inevitable, and therefore we should prepare for it (whatever it is).

Few will deny that the marriage of the computer and communications technologies will have a noticeable effect on occupational structures, industrial and office productivity, employment opportunities, and everyday life. However, acknowledging this effect does not automatically allow us to assert that we are in the throes of an 'information revolution' that will rival the Industrial Revolution's impact or that major qualitative changes in social relations will occur as a result of this effect. What is still in the balance is whether the stock of information will exceed that of misinformation, or vice versa.

This sceptical perspective is grounded in a more general outlook concerning the nature of major public policy issues in society today. This outlook in turn is based on the conviction that it is not new technologies, or the 'new possibilities' for action embodied therein, that do or will govern the definition of those issues or our responses to them. Rather, our political debate increasingly will be dominated by what may be called 'allocative' issues, and the solutions to them, such as they are, have zero-sum characteristics.[13] Examples are in-

come policy, national versus regional interests, and the relation between employment and social status: in such matters, individuals
and groups who increase their advantages vis-à-vis others do so by
decreasing the existing shares of others. Thus we are back to where
we started in this book, at Francis Bacon's illusionary premise that
technological progress would displace, once and for all, zero-sum
solutions to social conflict.

The great task for public policy today is to assist us in finding
reasonably civilized ways of dealing with allocative issues. If we can
do so, we will discover that managing the social impact of new
technologies is by comparison mere child's play.

10
CONCLUSION:
MANAGING TECHNOLOGIES

The preceding chapters may be taken as a series of
case studies about our collective fascination with
the products of scientific and technological innovation – and about
our inability to exorcise our persistent anxiety over whether those
products can lead us into the promised land of universal abundance
and contentment. We have dreamed of complete mastery over the
environment springing from our science and its instruments, enabling
us to harness all matter and energy to our desires, and giving us finally
the capacity to engineer life itself, thereby putting the evolutionary
fate of all existing species, as well as new ones designed to our
specifications, at our disposal.

We also have recurring nightmares: inexplicably we lose control
over the process of technological change. Our instruments appear
to take on a life of their own and lead us to a place where things are
not at all as we expected, or desired, and, moreover, where there are
no markers showing us the way back. I understand these fantasies
about autonomous technology to be a metaphor about the paradox
of control with respect to the relation between humanity and nature:
the instrumentalities furnished by modern science and technology,
which finally appeared to realize humanity's long-sought mastery
over its external environment, turn the species' own lack of self-
control into the means for an orgy of environmental degradation and
intraspecies violence that threatens its own viability.

Bacon's Wager

We end where we began, with Francis Bacon's wager. Bacon urged his contemporaries to take a chance on the immense benefits that sustained technological innovation would bring to society as a whole. He acknowledged that the enlarged human powers won through artful control over natural forces could be used for destructive or mischievous ends. But, he argued, the scale of the risk paled in comparison with the immensity of the promised benefits, and thus it was a risk well worth taking. Besides, there was a good way to manage the risk: in a famous passage in *The New Organon*, he reassured his readers that 'sound reason and true religion' would guarantee that human power over nature would be exercised responsibly.

Over the ensuing centuries, established religions were displaced in industrialized societies as guarantors of responsible behaviour in such matters. Instead, the effort to manage the risks stemming from technological applications has been internalized within the interactions between science and society.[1]

In a number of important senses, managing the process of technological innovation in modern industrial societies is nothing but the assessment, communication, and management of risks. Through an understanding of the nature and consequences of risks, governments, businesses, and the public seek to monitor and control those industrial products and practices that are potentially harmful to human health, to the well-being of other species, and to ecosystem functions. These attempts are classified under a variety of headings – most commonly, risk assessment or risk analysis, risk perception and acceptable risk, risk communication, and risk management.

Managing the risks associated with technological innovations in practice means both government and individuals making difficult choices on highly complex matters. Industries, regulatory authorities, and citizens must determine levels of acceptable risk for environmental and health hazards – for instance, those caused by toxic chemicals. They do so through such operations as choosing appropriate extrapolation models to estimate human health risks on the basis of animal test data. All parties must also make choices about how to balance estimated health and environmental risks against the estimated economic and social benefits to be derived from using toxic chemicals, knowing fully that new information may prove certain earlier choices incorrect.

For members of the public, managing the process of technological innovation means making choices about the truly bewildering array of risks present in industrial societies, both voluntary (such as smoking or skiing) and involuntary (such as airborne lead or occupational hazards). This means, among many other things, deciding how to regulate one's exposure to voluntary risks, how to rank risks in relation to each other, and how much governments should regulate hazardous products and processes and should spend on reducing risks associated with them.

During the first few months of 1989, for example, there were significant public controversies in North America about a variety of health and environmental risks. There were widespread reports of contamination of food supplies by pesticide residues, leading to estimates in the daily press of a significant number of additional deaths from cancer for the population as a whole. Controversy over a chemical (alar) used as a growth regulator for apples was even more animated, because children appeared especially at risk as a result of their heavy consumption of apple juice. And the massive Alaskan oil spill highlighted the risks of catastrophic environmental damage to animal species and economic losses to fisheries industries.

The substances and practices that occasioned these controversies – chemicals used in agriculture and shipments of crude oil in supertankers – had all been subjected to some process of risk assessment before being allowed in use.

Assessing and Managing Risks

Risk is a function of both the nature of a particular hazard arising from a product, process, or natural occurrence and the probability (for a person or non-human species) of encountering that hazard and suffering an adverse effect. Identification of a potential hazard and of the nature and severity of the possible attendant health risks is the entry-point for the risk assessment process. Probability is a function of an organism's exposure but also depends on intensity of exposure as well as on the organism's susceptibility to specific chemicals. Both acute and chronic effects are investigated through studies in toxicology, epidemiology, and molecular chemistry.

Thus risk is a function of hazard plus exposure. *Hazard* has been defined as the adverse impact on health that can result from exposure to a substance; exposure, as contact between a substance and an individual or a population. (Note that we may refer to hazards to the environment as well, that is, to ecosystems and to plant and animal species.) Concentrations of environmental contaminants can now be detected at levels so low that they are difficult to imagine; for example, within the past year a new technology has made it possible to measure dioxins and furans at the level of parts per quadrillion.

Risk assessment or risk analysis attempts to provide scientific estimates of health and environmental risks and to identify sources of uncertainty inherent in scientific data. Many of these estimates start with animal test data – disease rates observed in rat or mice populations that have been administered certain doses of a chemical; then, complex mathematical models are used to make extrapolations to presumed human health effects, which may result from exposure to the chemical at various concentrations. The net result might be a judgment something like the following: 'Exposure of male employees, using formulation type 'f' (for example, granular substance) and following activity pattern 'a' (for example, applying the chemical by hand ten days in a year), who are wearing protective clothing of type 'w', is estimated to have a probability 'p' (say, a chance of one in a hundred thousand) of five additional cancers of type 'c' per lifetime, for the exposed population as a whole, using the full amortization model of exposure assessment and 100 per cent dermal absorption rate assumptions, with an uncertainty range of type 'u'.'' (The number of judgment parameters has been reduced in this example.)

So why incur the risk at all? Almost every potentially harmful substance or practice is employed because it is supposed that we derive concrete benefits from it. Agricultural chemicals kill insects that would otherwise devour the crop; crude oil must be transported from where it is found to where it will be used; thousands of hazardous chemicals are indispensable to the industrial processes from which emerge the consumer products we enjoy. Modern society fully accepts Bacon's wager: the benefits outweigh the risks, and the risks can be managed.

Estimating risks is a difficult and uncertain business, but for most of the dangerous substances used in industrial production every day we have no better information base. In any case, most of us cannot understand the methods used in scientific risk assessments, and we make many of our decisions about potentially hazardous activities or substances on the basis of our informal perceptions of the hazards in our environment.

Managing technologies is a task of almost unimaginable complexity for many reasons, chief among them the inherent difficulties in risk assessment. These difficulties include identification of hazards at low levels of concentration in the environment (now being measured in parts per trillion or quadrillion), the meaning of animal test data for human health effects, and uncertainties in extrapolations of effects. The inherently problematic character of risk assessments inevitably produces complications for risk management decisions based in part on those assessments.

A good example is the long controversy in Canadian regulatory practice over the herbicide alachlor. This pesticide, made by Monsanto primarily for controlling weeds for corn and soybean production, was originally registered for use in Canada in 1969. It is one of the chemicals caught up in the 1977 'IBT scandal,' which involved invalidation of scientific test data supplied to the US Environmental Protection Agency by International Biotest Laboratories, a private firm doing laboratory analysis under contract. The toxicological studies originally supplied by Monsanto had to be redone, but in the mean time the product was allowed to stay on the market.

New toxicological data were supplied to the Health Protection Branch of Health and Welfare Canada in 1982, and the branch's risk analysis of these data lead to its recommendation to Agriculture Canada that alachlor be deemed to pose an unacceptable risk to health. Agriculture Canada accepted this recommendation and cancelled the registration for alachlor in 1985. Monsanto appealed this decision and requested that a review board be set up under the terms of the Pest Control Products Act to reconsider the decision. A five-member board, including two distinguished Canadian toxicologists, was established and after lengthy deliberations (including fourteen months of hearings) reported to the minister of agriculture in October 1987.

Having reviewed a seventy-volume submission from Monsanto and hundreds of exhibits, and having heard testimony and cross-examination of all the regulatory officials involved in the decision, the board stated that it disagreed with the cancellation of registration. The board specifically challenged the interpretation of scientific data and the resultant risk analysis of alachlor made by the Health Protection Branch. These disagreements have posed a severe test for the regulatory system for pesticides in Canada.[2]

In a case such as alachlor, different choices about risk assessment techniques within communities of scientific experts – for instance, about the complex quantitative calculations used in determining acceptable risk – are openly disputed in regulatory, quasi-judicial, and judicial proceedings. In addition, choices among risk management alternatives are vigorously debated by various parties to hearings, including industry, user groups, expert witnesses, individuals, and environmentalist organizations, each speaking for itself or through lawyers. These debates cover the entire range of potential decision inputs: what is an acceptable level of risk; how benefits are assessed; how risks and benefits can be weighed in relation to each other, or indeed whether this is appropriate at all; how the regulatory system can guarantee a fair hearing to all interested parties; how members of the public can participate effectively; and so forth.

A case such as alachlor reveals that choices in managing technologies have rested on highly unstable foundations. The information base for environmental hazards (including our ability to detect them at lower and lower concentrations) is continually changing, yet it is not feasible to review earlier decisions – except when particular controversies erupt – made on the basis of less adequate knowledge. Also, public perception of risk is in flux – for example, new demands are put on governments as a result of media coverage of disasters, and yet the hazards that then gain additional resources may not be the ones most urgently requiring more attention. In addition, new industrial chemicals requiring regulatory approval arrive without interruption, along with requests for expeditious review so that they might be marketed at the earliest opportunity. Finally, there are often bitter disputes over how all such decisions should be made and by whom. And there are many other sources of instability as well.

The Century of Environmental Crisis

As the twentieth century draws to a close, the endemic struggle for political domination among land-based empires, which finally in the Second World War had reached truly global dimensions, appears to have run its course, stymied by the very technologies of destruction it brought into being. The entertainments afforded to military bureaucracies by localized conflicts remain, but only the most sanguine warmongers among us believe that there will be anything worth salvaging after general exchanges of nuclear weapons.

We stand at the threshold of a new era, which will be marked by environmental crises on a global scale. Some of them will be simply a function of pressures on environmental resources from a larger human population in the so-called economically underdeveloped world. In China and elsewhere, people will face the bitter truth that they have no hope of escaping the age-old scourge of inadequate satisfaction for basic needs via the route mapped out by the richer nations, namely, by squandering fossil-fuel energy and dumping their wastes wherever they choose. Other crises will stem from the accumulated global residue of centuries of earlier industrial development and environmental degradation – atmospheric pollution, toxic chemical wastes, climatic change, massive deforestation, loss of fertile soil, radioactive wastes, reduction of biotic diversity, ocean pollution, and contaminated freshwater supplies. These and other hazards will be the inescapable reality of everyday life in the twenty-first century.

Moreover, many of these threats are of such a massive scale, and have such momentum driving them, that *no* action we take now, no matter how drastic, and no existing or foreseeable political or technological remedy, no matter how sophisticated, can forestall their irresistible magnification. Nothing can stop the destruction of tropical forests in the near future, and we shall be fortunate to preserve a few specimens here and there for tourist attractions. If by some miracle *all* manufacture and uses of chlorofluorocarbons (CFCs) were halted today, the migration of CFC compounds already present at lower atmospheric levels to the upper atmosphere, and their destruction of ozone there, would continue for decades to come. Our existing technologies around the world are hooked on fossil-fuel energy sources, and no amount of alarm about global warming can cause an appreciable reduction in fossil-fuel use for many years.

In confronting such problems we will find that the risk assessment and risk management strategies we have in hand are, by and large, quite accomplished techniques for addressing very specific problems, one at a time, that are limited in scope. An example would be an estimate of the risks and benefits of a particular pesticide, considered all by itself, where reliable test data results have been obtained, and assuming that it will always be used in carefully controlled applications by persons who will take the required safety precautions. However, such risk estimates will always carry a measure of uncertainty, and there may be later evidence of environmental or human health hazards unforeseen because of incomplete knowledge.

But in the coming century of environmental crises we will be faced with many problems that do not have such neatly structured dimensions. The solutions we possess or can devise are mostly for single problems, but there are undoubtedly a host of synergistic effects among toxic agents of which we are only dimly aware. We can do nothing about some of the dangers that are painfully obvious, because of the momentum inherent in current uses. Above all, so many of our incipient crises are spread across nations whose economic, social, and political situations diverge sharply, and there are few grounds for being optimistic about forging a common front against them. Bitter complaints about international inequities attend every international conference on global environmental issues.

At some point, I suspect, we shall be brought to the brink of collective despair about the trajectory of modern civilization and about the paradox of control in the relation between humanity and nature that it set before us. The scientific and technical instruments themselves will be denounced, often and loudly, as the chief villains of the piece. There may be calls to begin the trek back across the historical threshold where Bacon stood and offered his wager.

We shall need every ounce of technological ingenuity and scientific understanding we can muster to pull us back from the abyss of irremediable environmental disaster. But there is no hope of healing so long as the illusion persists that those instruments themselves can bring about the harmonization of human interests.

NOTES

Preface

1 All chapters except the first contain some of my previously published or circulated materials, though often much altered. Chapter 2 relies primarily on 'The Social Function of Knowledge,' from M. McGrath, ed., *Liberalism and the Modern Polity* (New York: Marcel Dekker, 1978), 177–93, but with new introductory and concluding sections. Chapter 3 draws on parts of 'The False Imperatives of Technology' in D. Shugarman, ed., *Thinking about Change* (Toronto: University of Toronto Press 1974), 105–21. Chapter 4 appeared as 'Technology and Degeneration: The Sublime Machine' in J.E. Chamberlin and S.L. Gilman, eds., *Degeneration* (New York: Columbia University Press 1985), 145–64; it has had only minor revisions. Chapter 5 is based on a section of 'Things Come Alive: Economy and Technology as Modes of Social Reproduction in Modern Society,' in C. Belisle and B. Schiele, eds., *Les Savoirs dans les pratiques quotidiennes: recherches sur les representations* (Paris: Editions du CNRS 1984), 40–65, but extensively revised and with new material added. Chapter 6 appeared as 'Dominion over Nature and Respect for Nature' in V. Mathieu and P. Rossi, ed., *Scientific Culture in the Contemporary World* (Milan: Scientia 1979), 389–402, and is used here with some changes.

Chapter 7 is the major part, substantially revised, of 'Political Aspects of Environmental Issues' from W. Leiss, ed., *Ecology versus Politics in Canada* (Toronto: University of Toronto Press 1979), 256–79. Chapter 8 was first circulated in 1979, under the title 'A Value Basis for Conservation Policy,' as a document for Ontario's Royal Commission on Electric Power Planning and was extensively reworked for W. Dunn, ed.,

Policy Analysis: Concepts and Methods (Greenwich, Conn.: JAI Press 1986), 185–201; it has had further changes and additions for this volume. And Chapter 9 was first published as 'Under Technology's Thumb: Public Policy and the Emergence of the Information Society' in A. Brannigan and S. Goldenberg, eds., *Social Responses to Technological Change* (Westport, Conn.: Greenwood Press 1985), 165–181; it was revised, supplemented, and republished as 'The Myth of the Information Society' in Ian Angus and Sut Jhally, eds., *Cultural Politics in Contemporary America* (New York and London: Routledge 1989), 282–98, and most of the latter version appears here.

Chapter One

1 J.M. Robertson, ed., *The Philosophical Works of Francis Bacon* (London: George Routledge and Sons 1905), 257
2 The four idols are set out in sections 38–68 of the *New Organon*. There is a contemporary parallel in the literature on 'risk perception,' in which various types of popular misunderstandings of the nature of current environmental risks have been categorized. For example, see the exposition and references in Vincent Covello, 'Informing People about Risks from Chemicals, Radiation, and Other Toxic Substances: A Review of Obstacles to Public Understanding and Effective Risk Communication,' in W. Leiss, ed., *Prospects and Problems in Risk Communication* (Waterloo, Ont., 1989)
3 The attentive reader may wonder at this close fit with the Baconian tetrad. Bacon's own classification is rather loose, with many overlapping elements in the four categories.
4 See Douglas Torgerson, *Industrialization and Assessment* (Toronto 1980).

Chapter Two

1 W. Leiss, *The Domination of Nature* (New York 1972), chap. 3
2 R. Brickman, S. Jasanoff, and T. Ilgen, *Controlling Chemicals* (Ithaca, NY, 1985)
3 Sheldon Wolin, *Politics and Vision* (Boston 1960), chaps. 8 and 9. See also Ellen Wood, *Mind and Politics* (Berkeley and Los Angeles, 1972), and C.B. Macpherson, *The Political Theory of Possessive Individualism* (New York 1962).
4 Wolin, *Politics*, 302
5 E.A.J. Johnson, 'The Place of Learning, Science, Vocational Training, and 'Art' in Pre-Smithian Economic Thought,' *Journal of Economic History*, 24 (1964), 129, 142–4

6 Adam Smith, *The Wealth of Nations*, ed. E. Cannan (New York 1937), 265-6

7 J.-B. Say, *A Treatise on Political Economy*, trans. C.R. Prinsep (New York 1964), 201

8 John Stuart Mill, *Principles of Political Economy*, ii, ed. J.M. Robson (Toronto 1965), 42

9 Pierre N.V. Tu, 'The Classical Economists and Education,' *Kyklos*, 22 (1969), 714

10 Karl Marx, *Capital*, iii (Moscow, 1962), 81; *Theories of Surplus Value*, part i (Moscow, n.d.), 379

11 Marx, *Grundrisse*, trans. Martin Nicolaus (Harmondsworth 1973), 706. In Marx's own text (*Grundrisse der Kritik der Politischen Ökonomie* [Berlin 1953], 594), he inserted the English word 'knowledge' after the German 'Wissen,' and the phrase 'general intellect' is likewise in English. See generally 690-712 of the Nicolaus translation.

12 J.H. Schaar and Sheldon Wolin, 'Education and the Technological Society,' *New York Review of Books*, 13 no. 6 (9 Oct. 1969), 4

13 E.G. Mesthene, 'How Technology Will Shape the Future,' *Science*, 161 (12 July 1968), 138, 137

14 J.K. Galbraith, *The New Industrial State* (Boston 1967), 68, 69. See the excellent discussion in J.E. Meade, 'Is 'The New Industrial State' Inevitable?' *Economic Journal*, 78 (1968), 372-92.

15 L.K. Cadwell, 'Managing the Scientific Super-Culture: The Task of Educational Preparation,' *Public Administration Review*, 27 (1967), 128

16 P.F. Drucker, *The Age of Discontinuity* (New York 1969), xi

17 Caldwell, 'Managing,' 130

18 Z. Brzezinski, 'America in the Technetronic Age,' *Encounter*, 30 no. 1 (Jan. 1968), 22. For a fuller statement see his *Between Two Ages* (New York 1970), 10-14. There he notes (p. 11) that in the technetronic era the essential problem for education is 'to discover the most effective techniques for the rational exploitation of social talent.'

19 R.E. Lane, 'The Decline of Politics and Ideology in a Knowledgeable Society,' *American Sociological Review*, 31 (1966), 658, 659

20 Daniel Bell, *The Coming of Post-Industrial Society* (New York 1976), xii-xviii, 343-5, 358-64

21 Professors William N. Dunn (Pittsburgh) and Amitai Etzioni (Columbia) have written extensively on the theme of knowledge and society in a series of books. See also the journal *Knowledge*, edited by Dunn.

22 F.A. Hayek, 'The Use of Knowledge in Society,' *Individualism and Economic Order* (Chicago 1948), 77-91

23 John McDermott, 'Knowledge Is Power,' *Nation*, 208 no. 15 (14 April 1969), 450. See generally Andrew Hacker, *The End of the American Era* (New York 1970).

Chapter Three

1 Harvey Averch, *A Strategic Analysis of Science and Technology Policy* (Baltimore 1985)

2 *International Social Science Bulletin*, 4 (1952), 243–399

3 For example: Carl F. Stover, ed., *The Technological Order* (Detroit 1963); Donald Schon, *Technology and Change* (New York 1967); D. Morse and A.W. Warner, ed., *Technological Innovation and Society* (New York 1966); Eli Ginsberg, ed., *Technology and Social Change* (New York 1964). For an exhaustive but unselective bibliography of the older literature see Victor Ferkiss, *Technological Man* (New York 1969), 295–327.

4 Forbes, *The Conquest of Nature: Technology and Its Consequences* (New York 1968); Mesthene, 'How Technology Will Shape the Future,' *Science*, 161 (12 July 1968), 135–43, 'Technology and Wisdom,' in Mesthene, ed., *Technology and Social Change* (Indianapolis 1967), 57–62, 'The Role of Technology in Society,' *Fourth Annual Report 1967–1968*, Harvard University Program on Technology and Society, 41–74 (reprinted in *Technology and Culture*, 10 [1969], 489–513), and *Technological Change: Its Impact on Man and Society* (New York 1970); Galbraith, *The New Industrial State* (Boston 1967); Ellul, *The Technological Society*, trans. John Wilkinson (New York 1967). Ellul's book was first published in French in 1954 (*La technique*, Paris), but it attracted wide attention only in the 1960s. For other summations of this literature see F.R. Allen, 'Technology and Social Change,' *Technology and Culture*, 1 (1960), 48–59; and Irene Taviss, 'The Technological Society: Some Challenges for the Social Sciences,' *Social Research*, 35 (1968), 521–39.

5 The neologism is a product of technology and electronics: Zbigniew Brzezinski, 'America in the Technetronic Age,' *Encounter*, 30 no. 1 (Jan. 1968), 16–26.

6 Galbraith, *The New Industrial State*, chap. 2; Mesthene, 'Comment,' Symposium on the Role of Technology in Society, *Technology and Culture*, 10 (1969), 536; Ellul, *Technological Society*, 210 and elsewhere; Forbes, *Conquest* (pp. x, 75), speaks of an 'environmental imperative' to which human technology responds.

7 Forbes, *Conquest*, vii; Forbes takes great pains to distinguish his views from those of Ellul (*Technological Society*, 72–6), but this passage is perfectly in accord with Ellul's thesis!

8 See especially 78–147 of Ellul, *Technological Society*.

9 Mesthene, 'Technology and Wisdom,' 59.

10 Mesthene, *Technological Change*, 25; Galbraith, *Industrial State*, 24; Forbes, *Conquest*, x; Ellul, *Technological Society*, xxv–xxvi, 13–18

11 *Les conséquences sociales du progrès technique: méthodologie* (Brussels 1956), especially 124ff
12 Ellul, *Technological Society*, 44–60
13 Galbraith, *Industrial State*, 403
14 Mesthene, 'The Role of Technology in Society', passim. See George H. Daniels, 'The Big Questions in the History of American Technology', *Technology and Culture*, 11 (1970), 3 and 8.
15 This and the preceding quotation are from Mesthene, 'How Technology Will Shape the Future', 136.
16 On the last point see Mesthene, 'The Role of Technology in Society', 23–4, 62–3.
17 Mesthene, *Technological Change*, 60; 'Technology and Wisdom', 59. Ellul, *Technological Society*, 97
18 Donald Schon, *Technology and Change* (New York 1967), xiii
19 Tom Settle, 'The Rationality of Science *versus* the Rationality of Magic', *Philosophy of the Social Sciences*, 1 (1971), 173–94.
20 See further William Leiss, *C.B. Macpherson: Dilemmas of Liberalism and Socialism* (Montreal 1988), chap. 4.
21 Lynn White, Jr, 'Technology Assessment from the Stance of a Medieval Historian', *American Historical Review*, 79 (1974), 1–13, and *Medieval Society and Technical Change* (New York 1966)
22 Richard Salisbury, *From Stone to Steel* (London 1962)

Chapter Four

1 John F. Kasson, *Civilizing the Machine: Technology and Republican Values in America, 1776–1900* (Harmondsworth 1976), 162. References in the following paragraph in the text are to 164.
2 Calvin Tomkins, *The Bride and the Bachelors: Five Masters of the Avant-Garde* (Harmondsworth 1978), 168ff; quotation from 182
3 Cited by Kasson, *Civilizing the Machine*, 171; the illustration is reproduced on 167.
4 Cf. Robert Beum, 'Literature and Machinisme', *Sewanee Review*, 86 (1978), 216–44
5 *The Collected Essays, Journalism and Letters of George Orwell*, 4 vols., ed. S. Orwell and I. Angus (New York 1968), IV, 72–5. Zamyatin, a naval engineer by training, spent the period 1914–17 in England.
6 Sander L. Gilman, 'Seeing the Insane: Mackenzie, Kleist, William James', *Modern Language Notes*, 93 (1978), 871–87. Gilman notes that he borrowed the idea from Stephen Pepper's *World Hypotheses* (Berkeley 1966).
7 Langdon Winner, *Autonomous Technology: Technics Out-of-Control as a Theme in Political Thought* (Cambridge, Mass., 1977)

8 Cited in Leo Marx, *The Machine in the Garden: Technology and the Pastoral Idea in America* (New York 1964), 186; see generally 180 – 90. For the identification of industrialism and republicanism see Kasson, *Civilizing the Machine*, chap. 1.

9 John Ruskin, *Unto This Last* (1862), in *The Works of John Ruskin*, 39 vols., ed. E.T. Cook and A. Wedderburn (London 1903–12), xvii, 29–30

10 *Selected Writings of Herman Melville*, Modern Library (New York 1952), 202

11 Cited by Kasson, *Civilizing the Machine*, 228

12 Leo Marx, *Machine*, 230–2

13 *Emerson's Complete Works*, 12 vols. (Boston 1903–4), v, 166–7

14 Ronald Meek, *Social Science and the Ignoble Savage* (Cambridge 1976), passim

15 Adam Smith, *An Inquiry into the Nature and Causes of the Wealth of Nations*, ed. E. Cannan, (New York 1937), 734–6

16 This paragraph is based on Maxine Berg, *The Machinery Question and the Making of Political Economy, 1815–1848* (Cambridge 1980), especially chaps. 11–13; the phrase in quotation marks is from an 1830 magazine piece and is cited on 257.

17 Karl Marx, *Grundrisse: Foundations of a Critique of Political Economy (1857–1858)*, trans. M. Nicolaus (Harmondsworth 1973), 692–3, 705

18 Thorstein Veblen, *The Instinct of Workmanship and the State of the Industrial Arts* (New York 1964), 313–14

19 Thomas Carlyle, *Critical and Miscellaneous Essays*, 5 vols. (London 1899), ii, 59

20 Ibid., 60, 61

21 Emerson, *Works*, v, 103

22 Carlyle, *Essays*, ii, 81

23 Lewis Kamm, 'People and Things in Zola's Rougon-Macquart: Reification Re-humanized,' *Philological Quarterly*, 53 (1974), 100–9

24 Karl Marx, *Grundrisse*, 692

25 H. Bruce Franklin, *Future Perfect: American Science Fiction of the Nineteenth Century* (New York 1966), 145

26 In what follows I am indebted to two commentaries: William B. Dillingham, *Melville's Short Fiction, 1853–1856* (Athens, G., 1977), chap. 8, and Marvin Fisher, *Going under: Melville's Short Fiction and the American 1850's* (Baton Rouge, La., 1977), 70–94.

27 Reproduced in Kasson, *Civilizing the Machine*, 179

28 *The Collected Tales of E.M. Forster* (New York 1964), vii–viii

29 Yevgeny Zamyatin, *We*, trans. Mirra Ginsburg (New York 1972), 22

30 Ibid., 179–80

31 John Searle, 'The Myth of the Computer,' *New York Review of Books*, 29 no. 7 (29 April 1982), 3–6

32 Stanislaw Lem, *Mortal Engines*, trans. Michael Kandel (New York 1977); *The Cyberiad: Fables for the Cybernetic Age* (New York 1976)

Chapter Five

1 Marx refers to this reading and uses the term *fetish* in his series of newspaper articles (1842) on the 'Wood Theft Debates': E. Sherover, 'The Virtue of Poverty: Marx's Transformation of Hegel's Concept of the Poor,' *Canadian Journal of Political and Social Theory*, 3 (1979), 59 and n 7.
2 See Sut Jhally, *The Codes of Advertising* (New York 1987), chap. 2, for a fuller discussion of commodity fetishism, with references, and for a well-argued and different interpretation of Marx's notion.
3 For example, there is (so far as I know) only a single important reference in Marx's *Grundrisse* (1857–8): 'The crude materialism of the economists who regard as the *natural properties* of things what are social relations of production among people ... is at the same time just as crude an idealism, even fetishism, since it imputes social relations to things as inherent characteristics, and thus mystifies them.' *Grundrisse*, trans. M. Nicolaus (London 1973), 687
4 The word 'ungeheuer' also has other meanings – 'monstrous,' 'shocking,' 'astonishing,' and 'dreadful,' for example.
5 *Capital*, i, trans. Ben Fowkes (London 1976), 164–5
6 Ibid., 165
7 Georg Lukács, 'Die Verdinglichung und das Bewusstsein des Proletariats' (first published 1923), in *Geschichte und Klassenbewusstsein* (Neuweid and Berlin 1968), 257–397; English translation by R. Livingstone, *History and Class Consciousness* (Cambridge, Mass., 1971), 83–222. The best restatement is by Lucien Goldmann, 'La réification,' in his *Recherches dialectiques* (Paris 1959), 64–106. Cf. Andrew Feenberg, *Lukács, Marx and the Sources of Critical Theory* (Oxford 1981), chap. 3.
8 Marx, *Capital*, i, 165
9 Lukács, 'Die Verdinglichung,' 266 (English translation [modified], p. 91); for the reference to Marx, see *Capital*, i, 170. The *Muret-Sanders Dictionary* gives 'natural growth' and 'spontaneous' for 'naturwüchsig'; 'original,' 'native,' and 'natural' for 'urwüchsig.' Livingstone's translation gives 'natural' – in quotation marks – for both. Marx used the term *Naturwüchsigkeit* in *The German Ideology* and *Grundrisse*: 'The term itself denotes the quality of unplanned, spontaneous growth in uninterrupted continuity with nature – being rooted in or embedded in nature.' Jeremy Shapiro, 'The Slime of History,' in J. O'Neill, ed., *On Critical Theory* (New York 1976), 147. The connotations of these

terms are very close to those of the word 'autochthonous.'

10 Max Weber, *The Theory of Social and Economic Organization*, ed. T. Parsons (New York n.d.), 160ff. For an excellent commentary see Ian Angus, *Technique and Enlightenment* (Washington, DC, 1984), 67–86.

11 The references in the text are from Lukács, 'Die Verdinglichung,' 262–7 (English trans., 82–92); Lukács's way of contrasting 'mechanical' and 'organic' is the exact opposite of Durkheim's.

12 Georg Simmel, *The Philosophy of Money*, trans. T. Bottomore and D. Frisby (London 1978), 346

13 Marcuse, 'Some Social Implications of Modern Technology,' *Studies in Philosophy and Social Science*, 9 (1941), 414–39

14 *One-Dimensional Man* (Boston 1964), xv

15 Sartre, *Critique de la raison dialectique* (Paris 1960); English translation by A. Sheridan-Smith, *Critique of Dialectical Reason* (London 1976). The quotations are from 238, 246, and 285 (English trans., 170, 178, and 227).

16 Ibid., 138 (English trans., 45–6)

17 Ibid., 279 (English trans., 219)

Chapter Six

1 A useful summary of these themes is in John Passmore, *Man's Responsibility for Nature* (London 1974), chap. 1; but see especially the great work by Clarence Glacken, *Traces on the Rhodian Shore: Nature and Culture in Western Thought from Ancient Times to the End of the Eighteenth Century* (Berkeley, Calif., 1967).

2 The best account of these developments will be found in the two outstanding studies by Paolo Rossi, *Francis Bacon* (London 1968) and *Philosophy, Technology and the Arts in the Early Modern Era* (New York 1970).

3 J.M. Robertson, ed., *The Philosophical Works of Francis Bacon* (London 1905), 387

4 For references and further commentary see William Leiss, *The Domination of Nature* (New York 1972), chap. 3.

Chapter Seven

1 Barry Commoner, *The Poverty of Power* (New York 1976), 216

2 Anthony Downs, 'Up and down with Ecology – the Issue-Attention Cycle,' *Public Interest*, no. 28 (summer 1972), 38–50

3 Thomas Berger, *Northern Frontier, Northern Homeland: The Report of the Mackenzie Valley Pipeline Inquiry* (Ottawa 1977), i, 30

4 *Globe and Mail*, 9 Feb. 1977

5 Ibid., 4, 6, 7 Oct. 1975

6 See generally Liora Salter, *Mandated Science* (Dordrecht 1988).
7 C.H. Enloe, *The Politics of Pollution in a Comparative Perspective* (New York 1975); D.R. Kelley et al., *The Economic Superpowers and the Environment* (San Francisco 1976)
8 See W. Leiss, S. Kline, and S. Jhally, *Social Communication in Advertising* (Toronto 1986), especially chap. 4.
9 Berger, *Northern Frontier*, 94
10 See further the writings of Holmes Rolston III – for example, *Philosophy Gone Wild: Essays in Environmental Ethics* (Buffalo, NY, 1986), and especially Neil Evernden, *Natural Alien* (Toronto 1984).

Chapter Eight

1 Albert Borgmann, *Technology and the Character of Contemporary Life* (Chicago 1984)
2 This is developed more fully in William Leiss, *The Limits to Satisfaction: An Essay on the Problem of Needs and Commodities* (Montreal 1988).
3 W. Leiss, S. Kline, and S. Jhally, *Social Communication in Advertising* (Toronto 1986); R.W. Fox and T.J.J. Lears, eds., *The Culture of Consumption* (New York 1983)
4 Tibor Scitovsky, *The Joyless Economy* (New York 1976), 161–5
5 Ibid.; Albert O. Hirschman, *Shifting Involvements* (Princeton 1982); Leiss, *Limits to Satisfaction*
6 Peter Penz, *Consumer Sovereignty and Human Interests* (Cambridge 1986)
7 My suggestion about a new phase has been informed in part by the hypothesis of internal social limits to social and economic 'progress,' as defined by the conventional, quantitatively expressed indicators. This is the theme of Fred Hirsch's *Social Limits to Growth* (Cambridge, Mass., 1976) and Lester Thurow's *The Zero-Sum Society* (New York 1980).
8 A. Mitchell, *The Nine American Lifestyles* (New York 1983), part IV, lends some support to this expectation.
9 This discussion was inspired by Milton Mayeroff's fine book, *On Caring* (New York 1971).
10 The implicit framework is the 'value-critical approach' defended by Martin Rein in both *Social Science and Public Policy* (Harmondsworth 1976) and *From Policy to Practice* (Armonk, NY, 1983).
11 Cf. M. Csikszentmihalyi and E. Rochberg-Halton, *The Meaning of Things: Domestic Symbols and the Self* (New York 1981), especially 195: 'The perceptive self is one capable of aesthetic experience and can allow the intrinsic qualities of an object or situation to be fully realized in the interpretation.'

12 Borgmann, *Technology*, 81, 182ff
13 L. Schipper and J. Darmstadter, 'The Logic of Energy Conservation,' *Technology Review*, no. 80 (Jan. 1978), 41–50
14 Scitovsky, *The Joyless Economy*; Hirschman, *Shifting Involvements*; R.P. Coleman and L. Rainwater, *Social Standing in America* (New York 1978)

Chapter Nine

1 S. Serafini and M. Andrieu, Department of Communications, Government of Canada, *The Information Revolution and Its Implications for Canada* (Ottawa 1981), 13
2 Arthur Cordell, Science Council of Canada, *The Uneasy Eighties: The Transition to an Information Society* (Ottawa 1985), 3
3 Kimon Valaskakis, *The Information Society: The Issues and the Choices*, Integrating Report for the Information Society Project, Department of Communications (Ottawa 1979), 40
4 M.U. Porat, *The Information Economy*, 9 vols., Office of Telecommunications, Special Project 77-12 (Washington, DC, 1977)
5 Daniel Bell, *The Coming of Post-Industrial Society* (New York 1973), 14. With the following discussion cf. Krishan Kumar, *Prophecy and Progress* (Harmondsworth 1978), chap. 6; and Peter Cook, 'The Informed Citizen: Technology and Responsibility in the Information Society,' PHD thesis, Simon Fraser University, 1989.
6 Bell, *Post-Industrial Society*, 137
7 Ibid., 43
8 Serafini and Andrieu, *Revolution*, 19
9 Valaskakis, *The Information Society*, 40; Serafini and Andrieu, *Revolution*, 8
10 See generally Jonathan Kozol, *Illiterate America* (New York 1985).
11 Edwin Diamond and Stephen Bates, *The Spot: The Rise of Political Advertising on Television* (Cambridge, Mass., 1984); Joshua Meyerowitz, *No Sense of Place* (New York 1985), chap. 14
12 *Newsweek*, 10 Aug. 1987, 17
13 Lester Thurow, *The Zero-Sum Society* (New York 1980)

Chapter Ten

1 See Liora Salter, ed., *Managing Technology* (Toronto 1989).
2 Agriculture Canada, 'The Report of the Alachlor Review Board' (Ottawa 1987). See generally Law Reform Commission of Canada, *Pesticides in Canada: An Examination of Federal Law and Policy* (Ottawa [1987]).

BIBLIOGRAPHY

Allen, F.R. 'Technology and Social Change.' *Technology and Culture* 1 (1960), 48–59

Angus, Ian. *Technique and Enlightenment*. Washington, DC: University of America Press 1984

Averch, Harvey. *A Strategic Analysis of Science and Technology Policy*. Baltimore: Johns Hopkins University Press 1985

Bacon, Francis. *The Philosophical Works of Francis Bacon*. Ed. J.M. Robertson. London: George Routledge and Sons 1905

Bell, Daniel. *The Coming of Post-Industrial Society: A Venture In Social Forecasting*. New York: Basic Books 1973

Berg, Maxine. *The Machinery Question and the Making of Political Economy 1815–1848*. Cambridge: Cambridge University Press 1980

Berger, Thomas. *Northern Frontier, Northern Homeland: Report of the Mackenzie Valley Pipeline Inquiry*. Vol I. Ottawa: Ministry of Supply and Services 1977

Bernard, Stéphane. *Les conséquences sociales du progrès technique: methodoiogie*. Brussels: Editions du Parthenon 1956

Beum, Robert. 'Literature and *Machinisme*.' *Sewanee Review* 86 (1978), 216–44

Borgmann, Albert. *Technology and the Character of Contemporary Life: A Philosophical Inquiry*. Chicago: University of Chicago Press 1984

Brickman, Ronald, S. Jasanoff, and T. Ilgen. *Controlling Chemicals: The Politics of Regulation in Europe and the United States*. Ithaca, NY: Cornell University Press 1985

Brzezinski, Zbigniew. 'America in the Technetronic Age.' *Encounter* Jan. 1968, 22

– *Between Two Ages: America's Role in the Technetronic Era*. New York: Viking Press 1970

Caldwell, L.K. 'Managing the Scientific Super-Culture: The Task of Educational Preparation.' *Public Administration Review* 27 (1967), 128

Canada, Department of Agriculture. 'Report of the Alachlor Review Board.' Ottawa: Ministry of Supply and Services 1987

Canada, Law Reform Commission. *Pesticides in Canada: An Examination of Federal Law and Policy*. Montreal: Ministry of Supply and Services 1987

Carlyle, Thomas. *Critical and Miscellaneous Essays*. 5 vols. London: Chapman & Hall 1899

Coleman, Richard P., and Lee Rainwater. *Social Standing in America: New Dimensions of Class*. New York: Basic Books 1978

Commoner, Barry. *The Poverty of Power*. New York: Knopf 1976

Cook, Peter. 'The Informed Citizen: Technology and Responsibility in the Information Society.' Dissertation, Simon Fraser University 1989

Cordell, Arthur. *The Uneasy Eighties: The Transition to an Information Society*. Ottawa: Science Council of Canada 1985

Covello, Vincent. 'Informing People About Risks from Chemicals, Radiation, and Other Toxic Substances: A Review of Obstacles to Public Understanding and Effective Risk Communication.' In William Leiss, ed. *Prospects and Problems in Risk Communication*. Waterloo: University of Waterloo Press 1989

Csikszentmihalyi, Mihaly, and Eugène Rochberg-Halton. *The Meaning of Things: Domestic Symbols and the Self*. New York: Cambridge University Press 1981

Daniels, George H. 'The Big Questions in the History of American Technology.' *Technology and Culture* 11 (1984), 3–15

Diamond, Edwin, and Stephen Bates. *The Spot: The Rise of Political Advertising on Television*. Cambridge: MIT Press 1984

Dillingham, William B. *Melville's Short Fiction 1853–1856*. Athens, Georgia: University of Georgia Press 1977

Downs, Anthony. 'Up and Down with Ecology–The Issue-Attention Cycle.' *Public Interest* 28 (1982), 38–50

Drucker, Peter. *The Age of Discontinuity: Guidelines to Our Changing Society*. New York: Harper & Row 1969

Ellul, Jacques. *La technique: ou, l'enjeu du siècle*. Paris: A. Colin 1954
– *The Technological Society*. Trans. John Wilkinson. New York: Knopf 1964

Emerson, Ralph Waldo. *Emerson's Complete Works*. 12 vols. Boston: Houghton Mifflin 1903–4

Enloe, Cynthia. *The Politics of Pollution in a Comparative Perspective: Ecology and Power in Four Nations*. New York: McKay 1975

Evernden, Neil. *Natural Alien: Humankind and Environment*. Toronto: University of Toronto Press 1984

Feenberg, Andrew. *Lukács, Marx and the Sources of Critical Theory*. Oxford: Martin Robertson 1981

Ferkiss, Victor. *Technological Man: the Myth and the Reality*. New York: Braziller 1969

Fischoff, Baruch, et al. *Acceptable Risk*. Cambridge: Cambridge University Press 1981

Fisher, Marvin. *Going Under: Melville's Short Fiction and the American 1850's*. Baton Rouge: Louisiana State University Press 1977

Forbes, Robert. *The Conquest of Nature: Technology and Its Consequences*. New York: Praeger 1968

Forster, Edward M. *The Collected Tales of E.M. Forster*. New York: Knopf 1964

Fox, Richard, and T.J. Jackson Lears, eds. *The Culture of Consumption: Critical Essays in American History*. New York: Pantheon Books 1983

Franklin, H. Bruce. *Future Perfect: American Science Fiction of the Nineteenth Century*. New York: Oxford University Press 1966

Galbraith, John Kenneth. *The New Industrial State*. Boston: Houghton Mifflin 1967

Gilman, Sander L. 'Seeing the Insane: Mackenzie, Kleist, William James.' *Modern Language Notes* 93 (1978), 871–87

Ginsberg, Eli, ed. *Technology and Social Change*. New York: Columbia University Press 1964

Glacken, Clarence. *Traces on the Rhodian Shore: Nature and Culture in Western Thought from Ancient Times to the End of the Eighteenth Century*. Berkeley: University of California Press 1967

Globe and Mail. 4, 6, 7, Oct. 1975, 9 Feb. 1977

Goldmann, Lucien. *Recherches dialectiques*. Paris: Gallimard 1959

Hacker, Andrew. *The End of the American Era*. New York: Atheneum 1970

Hayek, Fredrick A. *Individualism and Economic Order*. Chicago: H. Regnery Co. 1948

Hirsch, Fred. *Social Limits to Growth*. Cambridge: Harvard University Press 1976

Hirschman, Albert O. *Shifting Involvements: Private Interest and Public Action*. Princeton: Princeton University Press 1982

International Social Science Bulletin 4 (1952), 243–399

Jhally, Sut. *The Codes of Advertising: Fetishism and the Political Economy of Meaning in the Consumer Society*. New York: St. Martin's Press 1987

Johnson, E.A.J. 'The Place of Learning, Science, Vocational Training, and "Art" in Pre-Smithian Economic Thought.' *Journal of Economic History* 24 (1964), 129–43

Kamm, Lewis. 'People and Things in Zola's Rougon-Macquart: Reification Re-humanized.' *Philological Quarterly* 53 (1974), 100–9

Kasson, John F. *Civilizing the Machine: Technology and Republican Values in America 1776-1900*. Harmondsworth: Penguin 1976

Kelley, Donald R., et al. *The Economic Superpowers and the Environment: the United States, the Soviet Union and Japan*. San Francisco: W.H. Freeman 1976

Kozol, Jonathan. *Illiterate America*. New York: Anchor Press/Doubleday 1985

Kumar, Krishan. *Prophecy and Progress: The Sociology of Industrial and Post-Industrial Society*. Harmondsworth: Penguin 1978

Lane, R.E. 'The Decline of Politics and Ideology in a Knowledgeable Society.' *American Sociological Review* 31 (1966), 644-60

Leiss, William. *C.B. Macpherson: Dilemmas of Liberalism and Socialism*. Montreal: New World Perspectives 1988

– *The Domination of Nature*. New York: Braziller 1972

– *The Limits to Satisfaction: An Essay on the Problem of Needs and Commodities*. Toronto: University of Toronto Press 1976

Leiss, William, Stephen Kline, and Sut Jhally. *Social Communication in Advertising*. Toronto: Methuen 1986

Lem, Stanislaw. *The Cyberiad: Fables for the Cybernetic Age*. Trans. Michael Kandel. New York: Seabury Press 1974 (1976)

– *Mortal Engines*. Trans. Michael Kandel. New York: Seabury Press 1977

Lukács, Georg. *Geschichte und Klassenbewusstsein*. Neuweid and Berlin: Luchterhand 1968. Trans. Livingstone, Rodney. *History and Class Consciousness: Studies in Marxist Dialectics*. Cambridge: MIT Press 1971

McDermott, John. 'Knowledge Is Power.' *The Nation* 14 Apr. 1969, 450

Macpherson, Crawford B. *The Political Theory of Possessive Individualism: Hobbes to Locke*. Oxford: Clarendon Press 1962

Marcuse, Herbert. *One-Dimensional Man: Studies in the Ideology of Advanced Industrial Society*. Boston: Beacon Press 1964

– 'Some Social Implications of Modern Technology.' *Studies in Philosophy and Social Science* 9 (1941), 414-39

Marx, Karl. *Capital: A Critique of Political Economy*. Vol. I Trans. Ben Fowkes. London: Penguin 1976. Vol III: Moscow: Progress Publishers 1962

– *Grundrisse der Kritik der Politischen Ökonomie*. Berlin: Dietz, 1953

– *Grundrisse: Foundations of a Critique of Political Economy (1857-1858)*. Trans. Martin Nicolaus. Harmondsworth: Penguin 1973

– *Theories of Surplus Value: Volume IV of Capital*. Part i. Trans. Emile Burns. Ed. S. Ryazanskaya. Moscow: Progress Publishers 1969

Marx, Karl, and Frederick Engels. *The German Ideology*. Ed. C.J. Arthur. Parts i-iii, with 'Introduction to a Critique of Political Economy.' London: Lawrence & Wishart 1974

Marx, Leo. *The Machine in the Garden: Technology and the Pastoral Idea in America*. New York: Oxford University Press 1964

Mayeroff, Milton. *On Caring*. New York: Harper & Row 1971

Meade, J.E. 'Is 'The New Industrial State' Inevitable?' *Economic Journal* 78 (1968), 372–92

Meek, Ronald. *Social Science and the Ignoble Savage*. Cambridge: Cambridge University Press 1976

Melville, Herman. *Selected Writings of Herman Melville*. New York: Modern Library 1952

Mesthene, Emmanuel. 'Comment: Symposium on the Role of Technology in Society.' *Technology and Culture* 10 (1969): 536; reprinted as 'The Role of Technology in Society' in *Fourth Annual Report 1967–1968*. Harvard University Program on Technology and Society.

– 'How Technology Will Shape the Future.' *Science* 12 July 1968, 137–8

– *Technological Change: Its Impact on Man and Society*. New York: New American Library 1970

– ed. *Technology and Social Change*. Indianapolis: Bobbs-Merrill 1967

Meyerowitz, Joshua. *No Sense of Place: The Impact of Electronic Media on Social Behavior*. New York: Oxford University Press 1985

Mill, John Stuart. *Principles of Political Economy*. Vol. ii of *Collected Works*. Ed. J.M. Robson. Toronto: University of Toronto Press 1965

Mitchell, Arnold. *The Nine American Lifestyles: Who We Are and Where We're Going*. New York: MacMillan 1983

Morse, Dean, and Aaron W. Warner, eds. *Technological Innovation and Society*. New York: Columbia University Press 1966

Muret-Sanders Encyclopaedic English-German and German-English Dictionary. 2 vols. Abridged ed. New York: Frederick Ungar 1931

Newsweek. 10 Aug. 1987, 17

Orwell, Sonia, and Ian Angus, eds. *Collected Essays, Journalism and Letters of George Orwell*. 4 vols. New York: Harcourt Brace & World 1968

Passmore, John. *Man's Responsibility for Nature: Ecological Problems and Western Traditions*. London: Duckworth 1974

Penz, Peter. *Consumer Sovereignty and Human Interests*. Cambridge: Cambridge University Press 1986

Pepper, Stephen. *World Hypotheses: A Study in Evidence*. Berkeley: University of California Press 1966

Porat, Marc U. *The Information Economy*. us Office of Telecommunications, Special Project 77–12. 9 vols. Washington: GPO 1977

Rein, Martin. *From Policy to Practice*. Armonk, NY: M.E. Sharpe 1983

– *Social Science and Public Policy*. Harmondsworth: Penguin 1976

Rolston, Holmes, iii. *Philosophy Gone Wild: Essays in Environmental Ethics*. Buffalo: Prometheus 1986

Rossi, Paolo. *Francis Bacon: From Magic to Science*. Trans. Sacha Rabinovitch. Chicago: University of Chicago Press 1968

– *Philosophy, Technology and the Arts in the Early Modern Era*. Trans.

Salvator Attanasio. Ed. Benjamin Nelson. New York: Harper & Row 1970

Ruskin, John. *The Works of John Ruskin*. 39 vols. Eds. E.T. Cook and A. Wedderburn. London: G. Allen 1903–12

Salisbury, Richard. *From Stone to Steel: Economic Consequences of Technological Change in New Guinea*. London: Cambridge University Press 1962

Salter, Liora. *Mandated Science: Science and Scientists in the Making of Standards*. Dordrecht: Kluwer Academic Publishers 1988

Salter, Liora. ed. *Managing Technology*. Toronto: Garamond 1989

Sartre, Jean Paul. *Critique de la raison dialectique*. Paris: Gallimard 1960
– *Critique of Dialectical Reason*. Trans. Alan Sheridan-Smith. Ed. Jonathon Ree. London: NLB 1976

Say, Jean-Baptiste. *A Treatise on Political Economy*. Trans. Charles Robert Prinsep. New York: A.M. Kelley 1964

Schaar, J.H., and Sheldon Wolin. 'Education and the Technological Society.' *New York Review of Books*. 9 Oct. 1969, 4

Schipper, L., and J. Darmstadter. 'The Logic of Energy Conservation.' *Technology Review*. Jan. 1978, 41–50

Schon, Donald. *Technology and Change: The New Heraclitus*. New York: Delacorte Press 1967

Scitovsky, Tibor. *The Joyless Economy: An Inquiry into Human Satisfaction and Consumer Dissatisfaction*. New York: Oxford University Press 1976

Searle, John. 'The Myth of the Computer.' *New York Review of Books*. 29 Apr. 1982, 3–6

Serafini, Shirley, and Michel Andrieu. *The Information Revolution and Its Implications for Canada*. Canada, Department of Communication. Ottawa: Ministry of Supply and Services 1980

Settle, Tom. 'The Rationality of Science versus the Rationality of Magic.' *Philosophy of the Social Sciences* 1 (1971), 173–94

Shapiro, Jeremy. 'The Slime of History.' In *On Critical Theory*. Ed. J. O'Neill. New York: Seabury Press 1976

Sherover, E. 'The Virtue of Poverty: Marx's Transformation of Hegel's Concept of the Poor.' *Canadian Journal of Political and Social Theory* 3 (1979), 59–70

Simmel, Georg. *The Philosophy of Money*. Trans. Tom Bottomore and David Frisby. London: Routledge and Kegan Paul 1978

Smith, Adam. *An Inquiry into the Nature and Causes of the Wealth of Nations*. Ed. Edwin Cannan. New York: Modern Library 1937

Stover, Carl, ed. *The Technological Order*. Detroit: Wayne State University Press 1963

Taviss, Irene. 'The Technological Society: Some Challenges for the Social Sciences.' *Social Research* 35 (1968), 521–39

Technology and Culture 10 (1969), 489–513

Thurow, Lester. *The Zero Sum Society: Distribution and the Possibilities for Economic Change*. New York: Basic Books 1980

Tomkins, Calvin. *The Bride and the Bachelors: Five Masters of the Avant-Garde*. Harmondsworth: Penguin 1978

Torgerson, Douglas. *Industrialization and Assessment: Social Impact Assessments as a Social Phenomenon*. Toronto: York University 1980

Tu, Pierre N.V. 'The Classical Economists and Education.' *Kyklos* 22 (1969), 714

Valaskakis, Kimon. *The Information Society: The Issues and the Choices*. Canada, Department of Communications, Integrating Report for the Information Society Project. Ottawa: Ministry of Supply and Services 1979

Veblen, Thorstein. *The Instinct of Workmanship and the State of the Industrial Arts*. New York: A.M. Kelley 1964

Weber, Max. *The Theory of Social and Economic Organization*. Ed. Talcott Parsons. New York: Free Press 1957

White, Lynn, Jr. *Medieval Technology and Social Change*. New York: Oxford University Press 1966

– 'Technology Assessment from the Stance of a Medieval Historian.' *American Historical Review* 79 (1974), 1–13

Winner, Langdon. *Autonomous Technology: Technics Out-of-Control as a Theme in Political Thought*. Cambridge: MIT Press 1977

Wolin, Sheldon. *Politics and Vision: Continuity and Innovation in Western Political Thought*. Boston: Little Brown 1960

Wood, Ellen. *Mind and Politics: An Approach to the Meaning of Liberal and Socialist Individualism*. Berkeley and Los Angeles: University of California Press 1972

Zamyatin, Yevgeny. *We*. Trans. Mirra Ginsburg. New York: Viking Press 1972

INDEX

MARASCHINO